On the Downhill Side

On the Downhill Side

*The Collected Poems
of William Hedrington*

EDITED AND WITH AN INTRODUCTION
BY MICHAEL SMITH

Shambling Gate Press
Hyattsville, Md.

Published by
Shambling Gate Press
3314 Rosemary Lane
Hyattsville, Maryland 20782
301-779-6863
www.shamblinggate.com

"Apple" originally appeared in *Antioch Review;* "Illness" originally appeared in *Armadillo;* "For My Grandfather" originally appeared in *Westigan Review of Poetry;* "The Voices," "Walking Fence," and "Locked In" originally appeared in *New Collage.*

The publishers have been unable to identify every journal that originally published poems in this collection; we apologize to those we have omitted.

Design by Cheryl W. Hoffman

Library of Congress Control Number: 2001095655

ISBN 0-9679728-1-7

Printed in Canada

Printed on acid-free paper that meets the American National Standards Institute Z39-48 standard.

Contents

Contents

Other Poems

Contents

Publisher's Note

As Michael Smith says in his introduction, "here we are, all present and sober, an editor and publisher . . ." Like Michael, the editor of this collection, we were good friends of Bill Hedrington, although we scarcely knew Michael. This is characteristic, for Bill's friendships bridged worlds that managed to exist in complacent ignorance of each other, even in such a tiny universe as our alma mater, New College. It's tempting to say that this book should have been published years ago, but a project sometimes has to find its own time, and this is most assuredly the time for *On the Downhill Side*. We're very proud to have played a part in bringing it about.

A note on the text: A collection of poems entitled "On the Downhill Side" was put together by Bill in 1970. Because this is a title that we know met with Bill's approval, we have used it for the overall collection, although we have divided the poems into two sections to show which poems Bill had selected for a book he clearly intended for publication.

Bill was never satisfied with his work and constantly rewrote it, although he retained previous drafts. The sometimes daunting task of putting together a definitive version of Bill Hedrington's poetry was entrusted to Michael Smith by Darlene Knudtson, Bill's foster sister, on behalf of the family. Darlene and her husband, Ed, also supplied much of the material for the memoir of Bill in this volume. We owe them all a great debt of gratitude.

Cheryl White Hoffman
Lawrence Paulson

Introduction

Bill would not have approved of this memoir. But that was thirty years ago; he was twenty-three when he died. Young men think they're immortal, whether they admit it or not, and striking a pose is the most important thing there is—far more important than survival. Bill's stance—not a bad one, of course—was elusiveness, self-containment, unknowability. The Fortress of Solitude: every boy's fantasy. Bill had a much more imposing and better appointed Fortress than the rest of us boys. We all admired him hugely for it, and I still feel a superstitious reluctance to trespass, though the owner is long gone and past caring.

We have his poems. The Bill I knew, thirty years ago, would have said that should be enough. I'm not sure he really meant it: even the misanthropic dragon Fafner sings a little message for posterity with his last diminished fifth. Bill himself kept an immense mass of papers—rough drafts, notes to himself, musings, comments on the people and events around him, even a journal. Some of this material—indeed, its very existence—suggests that he, like Fafner, may have had posterity in mind.

This doesn't do away entirely with my slightly uneasy conscience; but I have the benefit of thirty years' practice ignoring my scruples. Remembering our dead is something we do, not for them, but for ourselves. We don't like to let go, and why the hell should we?

And furthermore, I'm still a bit angry—a sure antidote for scruples. No, Bill, the poems aren't enough. For one thing, there aren't enough of them. And there aren't enough of them because you went and got yourself killed on the road; and I remember how you drove. To this loss, I am less reconciled with every passing year—another year of your friendship and your work that I won't have. So this is my revenge, if you like, and you can take your medicine meekly wherever you are. You are gone, and your friends now must make what we can of what little we have of you.

But I hope you don't mind *too* much.

∼

I knew Bill only in college. This was in the late sixties, a wild and won-
derful time, in spite of all its folly and absurdity. Our campus was a very
small one, though very up-to-date in its views, very countercultural, very
peace-and-love, very turned-on. It was in this turbulent but lively setting
that I came to know Bill Hedrington. He was a year ahead of me, so he
was already a biggish man on campus. My initial impressions were favor-
able but not overwhelming; it was only later, when I got to know him
better, that Bill's exceptional qualities became evident.

He was tall and lean. In repose his expression was slightly melan-
choly though not gloomy. He tended to duck his head a bit, to the point
that the phrase "hang-dog expression" occasionally came to mind, and
habitually looked at the world from under lowered brows. His gait was
usually something between a slouch and a lope. His smile and laugh were
low-key, even shy, though he was not hard to amuse. In general, his man-
ner was contained and understated.

Whether one ought to call him handsome I don't know, but women
often found him attractive. His hairline had retreated a good deal,
although he was barely out of his teens; perhaps to compensate, he had
grown the world's most ridiculous pair of sideburns. Combined with his
somewhat abstracted expression, this gave him the air of a youthful,
earnest Civil War lieutenant from a Midwestern regiment who has had a
Rip van Winkle experience and awakened, inexplicably clad in cutoff
jeans and a T-shirt, at Woodstock. He tended to be laconic, but when he
did talk, he would really say something, instead of just dropping some
pregnant but noncommittal gnomism, as too many of us tiresomely did.

In spite of his tonsorial errors and attempts to be unobtrusive, he had
the knack, or the gift, of exerting a certain magnetism without overt
action: even when he was silent and still, you didn't overlook his presence
in a room. Of course we were all young and easily imposed upon, and of
course Bill had affected some fairly obvious Heathcliffian and Byronic
mannerisms. But Bill's charisma, for lack of a better word, went deeper
than that. One had the strong and, I still think, accurate sense that there
was a great deal going on beneath the surface.

Not my first memory of Bill, but one of the strongest: he reacted
badly to being startled. An instance: it's the college snack bar. Bill is stand-
ing at the counter, waiting for some frightful grilled thing to be dis-

gorged. I walk up behind him and speak, or tap his shoulder, or something, and he hasn't realized anyone is there. He whirls around in a flash, fist cocked back, apparently ready to throw a punch. He doesn't, fortunately—or do I mean, he doesn't, of course? Because I wondered then, and have often wondered since, was this for real? Or was it part of the pose? It certainly wasn't "cool" in any obvious sense.

Bill talked very little about his past and his family, so until it came time to write this memoir, I had very little sense of who he was before I met him. But it was definitely part of his persona that he came among us from a grittier, tougher world than the bland white-collar suburbia that bred most of us. And that was certainly true enough.

~

Chippewa Falls, Wisconsin, where Bill was born and did most of his growing up, got its start as a lumber town in the nineteenth century. Lumbering and the associated industries do not make for a delicate literary milieu. After the timber was all cut, other industries moved in. These too provided solid blue-collar jobs but didn't move the town very far from its working-class roots. Only in the last couple of decades has the ballyhooed postindustrial information economy had much of an impact on Chippewa Falls, and the town's original character is even now far from obliterated. It is a handsome town; the sawmills and the later industries attracted solid, hardworking people and paid solid wages; the people built solid, honest buildings and laid out wide, generous streets.

But its attractions were lost on me the first time I saw it, along with a carload of other friends of Bill's, at his funeral. No doubt it was partly the occasion, and partly the season, that made it seem so grim. Flat, bare, November-gray, and wet. Even in 1971 the primeval harshness of these glacier-scoured plains wasn't yet entirely obscured by creeping suburbia, and it must have been harsher still when Bill first saw that even, unblinking northern light, later in the year but very early in Henry Luce's "American century," on December 3, 1947, the son of Johanna Hedrington and an unknown father.

Johanna, it seems, was quite a girl. There was at least one other child, a daughter, also born without benefit of resident father. Johanna died in 1964, when Bill was in high school, and Bill wept for her. His feelings on that occasion must have been complex enough, because although he knew Johanna and she remained in the picture, she didn't raise him. That job was undertaken, as soon as the infant Bill got out of the hospital, by his uncle, Earl Hedrington, and Earl's wife, Clara. Clara already had two children, Darlene and Frank Newton, by her first marriage, and these two became for all practical purposes Bill's brother and sister, as Earl and Clara became his mother and father.

He came to Earl and Clara's household a far from unwelcome guest. Earl and Clara couldn't have children of their own, and they were devoted to Bill, as were Darlene and Frank. Clara's "whole world centered on Bill," says Bill's cousin Mary Makuski. And Mary remembers her mother saying that "Billy was Clara's whole life."

The household wasn't rich; Earl was employed for a while as a carpenter, but that seems to have been insufficiently dependable, so he took a job as a garbage collector. Frank and Darlene recall that the job carried some social stigma, but it paid the bills. The kids never went without anything they needed, and Clara "had her washing machines—always Maytags," Frank says. Cousin Mary says, "I enjoyed my time there—you had to toe the line but [Clara] was generous and giving." She also acknowledges that "if you didn't know her, you might have found her unpleasant," and indeed it seems clear that Bill's childhood wasn't altogether idyllic. The Earl and Clara family portrait has its darker shades.

For one thing, Earl and Clara drank. A boyhood friend of Bill's recalls that "their social life consisted mostly of going out every night and getting hammered." Darlene and Frank concur. Earl and Clara didn't drink at home, but just about every night they headed off after dinner to a convenient tavern and spent the rest of the evening there. During much of this time, Earl even had a second job tending bar in one of these establishments, the Indian Head; presumably this sideline made the drinking easier and less costly than it might otherwise have been.

Bill's younger cousin Peter wasn't aware of Earl and Clara's drinking, although he says that it doesn't surprise him: "All those people drank a lot back then." He does recall that the household didn't seem happy: "I didn't like going there. It wasn't a fun place. It seemed dark, closed in."

The Indian Head, where Earl and Clara spent their evenings, still stands. I was bold enough to drop in during a recent visit to Chippewa Falls. I felt a little conspicuous; the other patrons were decidedly a neighborhood crowd, and the attractive but tough-looking young cookie who served me my one draft beer didn't expend any effort pushing a second. But everybody was perfectly civil and the overall tone entirely benign.

Things might have been a bit different at a later hour, or in an earlier decade; at any rate, when Earl and Clara came home at the end of an Indian Head evening, they were combative—both with each other and with the kids. Frank, who was thirteen years older than Bill and already something of a Wisconsin Wild Child, would be awakened and roundly excoriated for his scrapes. Bill, who never got into scrapes and was apparently a model child, nevertheless was lectured on how grateful he should be for Earl and Clara's care.

They weren't altogether wrong about this, though most people would agree that they shouldn't have mentioned it. Yes, they drank, and yes, they were quarrelsome, but that's not all there was to them.

Clara, as we noted, had been married before, to Percy Newton, Darlene and Frank's father. He took off one day—"went out hunting and just didn't come back," says Frank, "and took all the change out of the Carnation Milk can before he left." There was "another woman in the picture," Darlene thinks, and Frank agrees that their father had "an eye for the ladies." Clara loaded her children into a little red wagon and pulled them down the road to her parents' house. The image is iconic: Clara was no weakling, she made do with what was at hand, and she put her shoulder to the wheel when she had to. People often had to, in the hard-bitten world of Chippewa Falls in the forties and fifties.

Clara seems to have been, if not a stronger character, then perhaps a more definite and decisive one than Earl. She was "headstrong," says cousin Mary. "She knew what she wanted and found ways to get it. She had a huge collection of salt and pepper shakers—she'd let you play with them, but she'd pick out the ones you could use."

But Earl was by no means an inconsiderable figure. Bill's cousin Peter actually has clearer memories of Earl than of Clara; he describes Earl as "not a very loose person—very controlled, not expressive, aware of himself." Earl had had a lengthy war. It appears that he was already enlisted in the 32d Wisconsin National Guard division (the "Red Arrow") when it was called to active duty in 1940, and he spent the rest of the war in uniform. The division compiled a very substantial combat record in the Papua, New Guinea, southern Philippines, and Luzon campaigns. Earl attained the rank of Tec 5, according to his gravestone, and also picked up malaria somewhere along the way. Another cousin, Dave, recalls that

Earl was not much given to discussing his experiences in the war; "I think he might have told one story, once," Dave says. Earl was still in uniform when he and Clara met. He was three years older than she was; both were in their thirties and had seen a fair amount of life, but their passion for each other seems to have been as fresh and strong as anything youth could offer. Cousin Mary remembers that they were "very close, very dependent on each other. Not on the surface. But it was like they were the only two people in the world." Did they argue? "Oh, yes, they did, but they didn't stay mad. Whenever I was there, they were always together."

There is a wonderful snapshot of them, taken at a county fair. Both are looking directly into the camera. Their expressions are unselfconscious and unstudied, though very far from childish. Earl is a striking-looking man; his face is almost gaunt, his eyes deep-sunk and, one feels, probably rather haunted in repose; a self-questioner and man of many second thoughts, though certainly no weakling. But in this image he is smiling, and his evident happiness is the more striking for being overlaid on his visible substratum of melancholy. Clara's face is immensely attractive: full and healthy looking, vigorous and in no way delicate, yet

intensely feminine; her troubles have taken away none of her youthful bloom. Her expression is less complex than Earl's but perhaps harder to characterize. She too is obviously happy—more than happy. One wants to use words like "triumphant" and "victorious," but these suggest a smugness that she doesn't have. She looks like a person who has found something very specific and important that she's spent a lot of effort searching for, and Earl is it, unlikely a candidate as he may appear, with his Epimethean pensiveness. Her clear-sighted gaze is full of strong intelligence. Proverbs notwithstanding, this is no blind love, and the force of her character comes across so strongly that we take a second look at Earl and half consciously defer to her judgment. Clara knows what she is about, and we cannot doubt that whatever she thinks she's found in Earl, it must certainly be there. Both of them have had their trials and lost their naïveté; yet they still have within them abundant springs of hope and vitality and look the future levelly in the eye. They were married on December 14, 1946.

Compare this image with another freezing Gorgon glance from that same future, taken a quarter-century later. It's their anniversary: December 1971. Bill's twenty-fourth birthday would have been a week or two before, but he has been dead a little over a month. Cousin Dave recalls that Clara was "just devastated" after Bill died. Cousin Mary says that "they all lived for each other—when [Bill] was gone they didn't want to be around anymore."

Characteristically, Clara's devastation is not evident in this picture. She and Earl are both wearing jackets, and Earl has a billed cap on; they're sitting at a Formica-topped table, in chairs with plastic upholstery. It's the old familiar Indian Head tavern, where Earl had tended bar, and Clara kept him company, for so many evenings. On the table in front of them, there's a lavish cake, surmounted by an escutcheon bearing the number 25. Wildly overexposed by the camera's flash, the cake appears radioactive. Is it made of Kryptonite? Is it responsible for what has happened to the handsome young couple from the county fair? Earl's gauntness is now nearly skeletal, and Clara's face is lined and puffy. They have turned away from the future's gaze and toward each other. Earl's eyes are downcast, his posture rather bent. Clara looks steadily into his face; one arm is flung around his shoulder, and her other hand is clasped in his. She is still smiling, but at him now, not at us. Her expression is no longer triumphant, but it is full of strong, steadfast, and time-defying tenderness. She seems to be protecting him, comforting him, perhaps cajoling him; at the same time she clings to him out of some great yearning of her own. He appears almost lost in his own thoughts, a man bowed down by years and burdensome reflections; yet his hand grips hers tightly. He does not merely allow her embrace, he meets it, in his own constrained and involuted way. The youthful heat of the earlier picture is long gone, but something stubborn and unquenchable still burns between these two.

Within a year, Clara too was dead; she lasted out one more hard

Wisconsin winter after losing Bill, and died amid the rich, brief bloom of a northern July. Earl soldiered on without her for another two years. We are somehow surprised to hear this; but there was always more to Earl than met the eye.

Indeed, he has a further surprise for us; after Clara's death he found himself a girlfriend. In the first phase of Earl's bereavement, his step-daughter Darlene had been helping him out with his checkbook and other small necessities, though she didn't have any great affection for him: "I did it for Mom's sake," she says. But once the girlfriend came on the scene, Darlene seems to have concluded that Earl was well able to take care of himself.

The girlfriend forms an interesting pendant to the story of Earl and Clara. Earl's ability to find company and solace with another woman doesn't detract from the importance of his relationship with Clara, but perhaps her departure created a little space for him to spread his wings for one last flight—she seems to have been a rather formidable person-ality. Earl may have felt a bit constrained when Clara was around; but at the same time, it certainly seems that she must have filled some deep need of his nature.

What might Bill have taken from these two? No doubt he learned caution. His contained, muted manner in later life probably owes much to Earl's example; self-protectiveness would have been vital in their household, subject as it was to boozy Sturm und Drang. He learned what it was to be loved, clearly, and learned what a complex and contradicto-ry blessing this can be. And he saw, as well, something of the strength and something of the travail that lies in the dialectic of men and women. An experience of love, then, and a capacity for it, and at the same time, a live-ly sense of its perils—these, perhaps, were some of Earl's and Clara's gifts.

$\approx$

There were other gift givers around Bill's cradle. Prominent among them were Frank and Darlene Newton, his foster siblings, allies, and protectors. They were thirteen and eleven, respectively, when he came on the scene. People nowadays might worry that they would resent the new arrival. In fact the result was quite the contrary.

Darlene says simply that "Bill was my baby," and there is, again, a pic-ture to illustrate the point. Darlene appears quite a competent young woman. Her air of maturity makes her look more grown-up than she could have been in fact. She is wearing a very fetching hat at a jaunty angle. Baby Bill is so wrapped up in blankets and sweaters and a sort of Teletubbies cap as to be a rather awkward burden, but Darlene has the situation under control. She is looking at him, and he is staring with infantine suspicion at the camera. A close look at her face reveals a complex expression; it seems happy but thoughtful. She is looking not just at Bill but also, one feels, past him. In a few years she will be holding her own babies and experiencing the joys and sorrows of motherhood in her own right. Is her veiled look the sign of a foreshadowing? In any case we can see that she has a gift for motherhood, and we think she will probably make a fine job of it, and knowing what we do about Clara in her motherly capacity, we are glad to see that she has this girl for a subaltern.

And then there's Frank. Frank was a handful as a child and grew up into a wild man. Rebellious, disobedient, combative, and constantly in trouble, Frank was the sort of boy that journalists and politicians nowadays consider a deep and puzzling social problem.

Chippewa Falls in the late forties and fifties, though, had its ways of dealing with boys and young men like Frank. He saw the inside of the local jail more than once—indeed, he got his name in the paper on one occasion as the "first customer" of the brand-new county lockup. But these were the days before American politics became the theater of punishment, with its elaborate apparatus of felon manufacture. Police and judges in Chippewa Falls had a lot of discretion, and at least in Frank's case they seem to have had a fair endowment of common sense to go with it. They didn't, apparently, classify him as some sort of alien being, requiring permanent quarantine like a deadly virus. Rather, one gets the impression that they had him sized up as a guy who would one day straighten himself out.

If so, their judgment was vindicated. Frank caused a lot of trouble and took a good many lumps; even his twenty months in Korea didn't settle him down, and he came home as wild as he left. But a point finally arrived in his life—it was, in fact, May 1, 1964—when he decided to change his ways. He stopped drinking and hasn't had a drop since. He moved with his wife, Donna, to Milwaukee and found a good steady job in a machine shop, which he kept for the next thirty years and more. This turn in Frank's life came at a crucial time for Bill, as we shall see.

Frank and Donna raised their children in Milwaukee and are now retired to the back of beyond in northern Minnesota. The wild man came in from the metaphorical woods, served his time as the solidest of solid citizens, and has now gone back to the literal woods. But his wildness is still evident. One has the sense, in his company, that this is a guy whom one would do well to treat with respect.

Frank now regrets that, as he says, "I wasn't much of a brother to

Bill." But I think he does himself less than justice. In talking with Frank and Darlene and Donna and Ed Knudtson, Darlene's husband, it becomes very clear that Bill was an unusual child: thoughtful beyond his years, solitary, and given to untypical pursuits. Such children are not always well tolerated by their coevals. Naturally I wondered whether Bill was teased or persecuted by other kids. Frank's unconsidered, even absentminded, answer was, "Oh, I wouldn't let nobody shit on him." It's hard to convey the matter-of-fact, unselfregarding tone of this remark. There was nothing remotely resembling bluster or braggadocio in it. It was impossible to doubt that it simply represented an offhand, by-the-way statement of the literal truth.

Once more, the camera comes to our aid. People with teenage sons will appreciate this image at its full value. In front of a tumbledown shed or barn stands Frank, about fourteen, wearing a high-school football uniform. His face is a bit puffy, eyes half shut, and his left hand is on his head, in an eloquent gesture. Is he actually hung over, at this tender age? Surely not; but knowing the kind of boy he was, we can't quite dismiss the thought. On his right shoulder, baby Bill is perched, nonchalantly held in place by Frank's right arm. Bill's expression is that of an infant rajah astride one of his favorite elephants. Frank looks tough and maybe a bit pugnacious, but he doesn't seem to mind the slightly out-of-character baby on his shoulder. On the contrary, he looks as if he carries a baby around on his shoulder most of the time—as if the baby lives there—as if he has a baby on his shoulder by way of variation on the proverbial chip. If he seemed slightly more conscious of the baby, one might imagine him saying, "Wanna make something of it?" But it seems more in keeping with his body language to write in Frank's dialogue balloon, "Baby? What baby? Oh, *this* baby! Hey, meet my brother Bill."

~

Now that we have the supporting cast on stage, let's do that: meet Bill, I mean, as much as we can.

One thing everybody agrees on: he was "smart." Frank, and Donna, and Darlene and Ed, and Bill's neighbor and boyhood friend, Jim Crandell, all cite this as the most striking thing about him. Jim says he would have expected Bill to grow up to be a scientist or an engineer. Cousin Mary would have expected a "nuclear physicist." He took an interest in mechanical things and, later, in electronics and became adept in both areas. His cousin Peter remembers a science-fair project in which Bill cultivated a tray full of four-leaf clovers; Peter thinks this may have received a prize, since Earl and Clara were "proud of it" and displayed the crop prominently in their living room. Bill always got good grades in school and was never a discipline problem, though cousin Dave recalls some mischievous rambles "down by the river," including occasional raids on a nearby watermelon patch.

Insofar as Earl and Clara were capable of undiluted pampering, they pampered Bill; Frank and Darlene bluntly say they "spoiled" him, though he apparently didn't take undue advantage. One spoiled-child trait he did acquire: he was a picky eater. Couldn't stand onions, and if he were served something with onions in it, he would patiently pick all the onions out, no matter how finely chopped. He seldom had occasion to do so, since as Darlene says, "they cooked what Bill liked." But the slightly compulsive capacity for taking pains, revealed in the onion picking, never deserted him. His habit of worrying at a poem in later life, covering sheet after sheet of multiply-folded paper with minor variations in a tiny, cramped scrawl, seems a kind of onion picking by other means, and in a different sphere.

Jim Crandell's first memory of Bill: he's under the outside stairs leading up to the Hedrington apartment (Jim's family lives on the first floor). Bill is patiently constructing an elaborate system of roads and buildings through which to run his toy cars. Jim joins him, and this becomes a favorite game. Jim recalls that the building was the fun part; actually running the cars through the finished infrastructure was something of an anticlimax. (Bill and Jim seem to have discovered an important truth here, which also applies on a larger social scale.)

The two boys also played board games; Jim recalls one involving financial manipulation—"not Monopoly; something more complicated than that," God help us—and another involving military strategy. And they watched a lot of TV, which does not seem to have rotted the brain of either child. Perhaps TV was less perfected in those innocent days.

Bill didn't have a lot of friends, as a child or as a teenager, and Jim can't recall that he ever dated. (He made up handsomely for the latter omission in college.) He was, from the first, an inward sort of child who kept his feelings, and, one imagines, many of his thoughts to himself.

Jim was an athlete and is now a successful and respected sportscaster in California. Bill didn't go out for school teams, but in unofficial sports after school, Jim says Bill was "right there." Was he any good? Oh, yes, says Jim, with the judicious, precise approbation of professional expertise, "He was pretty lean and pretty strong." Jim doesn't recall any teasing about Earl's occupation on the garbage truck. "Nobody had any money in that neighborhood, so who could talk?" he says. Possibly Darlene and Frank, being older, were more sensitive on this topic. Bill went to Catholic schools and Jim to public ones, and by the time they were in high school, they weren't seeing much of each other. There was no breach, Jim says, they just had different circles.

Bill once observed, apropos of his cradle Catholicism, that "you can put it in neutral, but you can't stop the engine turning over." How true it really was for him is difficult to say. He had an eye for the transcendent, but was this because of, or in spite of, his early experience of religion? Certainly his researches in this area mostly expressed themselves in a very different idiom. But some of his musings on the Big Questions suggest that these questions first lodged themselves in his brain as posed by the astute old Roman firm. One of his own journal entries, from his college years, notes, "It's strange how deeply early religious training affects one."

The engine of Catholicism in Bill's household was Clara. Though she didn't go to Mass herself (because of her second marriage, perhaps?), she saw to it—or tried to see to it—that her kids did. Needless to say, Frank found ways to play hooky and sometimes persuaded Darlene to do so too. Bill was too young to join much in these delinquencies.

We have, again, a picture: Bill's First Communion, in 1957. Bill, ten or so, is neatly dressed though not Fauntleroyed, as happens with First Communions in less stern milieux. He's standing in a backyard, holding a candle and a missal. Clara stands behind him; she's bending over and embracing him, in an oddly stiff and restrained way. Does she feel that her little man has crossed a threshold and can no longer be subjected to a fully maternal hug? Or has this just become her style? Her expression seems severe, but a magnifying glass suggests that this appearance is largely due to a remarkably unbecoming pair of eyeglasses, in that diagonal teardrop shape popular in the fifties, with its sharply pointed, reptilian or bat-winged outer corners. Magnifying further, until the grain of the print begins to swarm like a plague of locusts over all the imaged features, do we see, behind these frightening space-alien goggles, a gleam of the old warmth we know from earlier days? Or do we just want to see it?

The little man's own expression is a study. He too stands rather stiffly, holding his book and candle in a reasonable approximation of the de rigueur hieratic pose. But his head is now bent, in that beetling way that became his habit later on, and he looks out at the camera from beneath distinctly lowered brows. His mouth, too, is set in a complex, ambiguous curve with which his friends became familiar in our college years: a crinkled, almost sinusoidal line. Not a grin, not a grimace, not a smile or a frown. Expressive, certainly, but of what? My reading of this look, in those later days, registered irony and a touch of self-mockery: a blend of rueful amusement and embarrassment. Apparently Bill started working on this stance rather early on.

In all these old pictures, Bill is elusive. To be sure, he seems happy. Would one see anything unusual in this boy, if one didn't know how he turned out—or rather, began to turn out? There is a hint of remoteness in some of the images. Though he usually looks very directly at the camera—an echo, here, of Earl and Clara's straightforward gaze—and though he is usually smiling, there is something about the eyes that suggests travel in realms far from Chippewa Falls.

The fact is, he seems to have been rather elusive even to those around him: right from the first, marked for an unusual destiny. Not that he was an oddball or a deviant or an outcast. Quite the opposite. His family and friends still speak of him with deep affection mixed with some degree of puzzlement. He was, it seems, not at all unavailable in spite of his solitary quality. His virtual nieces and nephews, the children of Darlene and Ed and Donna and Frank, remember him fondly as a perfectly satisfactory young uncle. They enjoyed teasing him and he took it good-naturedly. And his cousins Peter and Dave remember that he was kind to them, though he was a teenager and they were much younger. "He had an elaborate model train setup," Peter recalls, "and he let us play with it. Told us not to run the trains too fast, but then he went off and left us to it." Cousin Mary recalls him as "friendly" and "good-natured" and says that "people liked him a lot. He was always tinkering or reading a book—never bored—always had something to do. He was quiet; he'd keep to himself and just listen, or read a book." Was he sad? Mopey? "No. He just seemed like someone who was always seeking to learn more—looking for his place in life."

He wasn't self-serious. His college friends were well acquainted with his capacity for taking a pratfall and then neatly fielding the joke. This capacity showed up early. With enduring delight, Donna tells a story about seeing adolescent Bill bump his head on a low garage doorway. He looked up and saw her watching, and commented, "The garage is sinking or I'm growing. Either way, it's scary."

Certainly the air of happiness that Bill mostly wears in his childhood pictures is not the whole story. Darlene says he had his darker moods, and he still had them, in spades, when I knew him. She goes so far as to say he was "depressed" a lot of the time, but if so, it seems to have been a more energetic variety of depression than most. He developed his habit of pacing early on and went for long runs in the evening. Frank thinks that by the time Bill was in high school, he was writing poems in his head while pounding along. Ah, those innocent days! Running is a more single-minded business now. But "just doing it" was never Bill's style.

Still, whatever angel wrestling he was up to behind what he later called his "high Shakespearean brow—and getting higher every day," little evidence of it ever showed externally. Melville—a favorite of Bill's— remarks somewhere, if I recall correctly, that the whale, like all things that are mighty, wears a false front to the common world. One hesitates to improve on Melville; but is "false" really quite right? Unrevealing, yes. And the smooth, blank cliff of the whale's apparent forehead is not a bad analogy for Bill's competently assembled, self-concealing self-presentation, with his real thinking- and feeling-works lying far behind the surface. But false? I think not. The more I learn lately of his early life, the more I think that even less of him was pose than perhaps we realized at the time.

~

By the time Bill was in high school, he seems to have found life at home increasingly hard. Frank and Darlene don't recall any particular casus belli, but Clara's bossiness and the beer-fueled histrionics after an Indian Head evening seem to have become more and more difficult to take as Bill grew toward adulthood. Finally, in the summer before his last year of high school, he moved out. At first he stayed with Darlene and her husband Ed in Chippewa Falls. But Clara put the kibosh on that arrangement in short order. Darlene says that Clara felt that it would reflect badly on her and Earl if Bill were living in a different household in the same town. It is a measure of Clara's force of character that everybody seems to have accepted her ukase; Bill moved right out of town, to stay with Frank and his wife Donna in Milwaukee, a couple of hundred miles away. This was a turning point for Bill in several ways; it almost seems that Earl and Clara did him as big a favor by driving him out as they had done, seventeen years before, by taking him in.

He seems to have recorded this moment in a quick draft of a poem, on one of the midden of paper scraps he covered with his sharply slanted, compressed handwriting:

I have fought you long, my mother, my father
In this comfortable room
With this brown carpet as a battlefield
And this dun couch my last retreat in tears,
Yet I will run, for neither a son
Who would be man nor a daughter who
Would be woman
Can lose these bloody wars.
But now the great conflict
The last battle
Will end in our hate
And I will run
Until I am safe with the distance.
Someday I will come
And speak to you again
When I can forgive
Your well-wishing chains.

Bill worked and reworked his poems. Many of the ones in this book grew from such kernels, often extending as far back in his life. But he never revisited this one.

~

Providentially, Frank had just made his own sharp turn from wild man to solid citizen. He and Donna were able to offer Bill a stable, affectionate home during this critical year. Bill enrolled in Pius XI High School, a large and deservedly well regarded Catholic institution. Nobody seems to know, now, how the tuition got paid; but somehow or other, Bill had gotten in every way into a much bigger pond than Chippewa Falls, and his good fortune stayed with him. At Pius XI, he found teachers who recognized and nourished his gift.

I haven't been able to find any of Bill's high-school teachers, though Father Robert Carney, the alumni director at Pius XI, did his helpful best to hunt them down. Thanks to Bill's pack-rat habits, though, we have a documentary record. It consists of some dozens of typed sheets, each bearing a poem or other writing exercise of Bill's, with comments by one or more or his teachers. Bill dated these sheets—sometimes, rather drolly, with eminently Catholic constructions like "ante May 15, 1965"—so we can even put them in order. The writing itself, to my eye and ear, gives little indication of what Bill would later achieve; but apparently he was lucky enough to find teachers with better ears, or eyes, than mine. Two different hands account for most of the comments.

The most striking of these is a bold, blocky, almost certainly feminine but by no means pretty, semicursive script with some very original ways of forming certain letters. It seems to belong to someone whose initials are SMH. Frank and Donna Newton had the impression that Bill's main patron and cheerleader at Pius XI was a nun; is this, then, "Sister M. H."? Let's hope so; the idea of Bill, who was something of a Don Juan when I knew him, embarked on a voyage of literary discovery with an obviously strong-minded and determined sister, imaginative but unsentimental, professionally chaste but probably unshockable—it's just too good to give up. It's the stuff of which movies are made.

Did Sister M.H. know what she was launching into the world? I bet she did. Let's hope Bill stayed in touch with her and sent her some of his later work. Judging from her comments, she would certainly have been pleased by it. Would the contrast between Bill's life and explorations and those of the convent chapel have bothered her? Not necessarily; people seek the cloister for all kinds of reasons, but SMH doesn't come across as the type who would do so from a fear of life.

Whatever the incongruity of their personal lives, it certainly seems that SMH either was very persuasive or had literary tastes that fell into a preordained harmony with Bill's own emerging outlook. One of her early comments on a Hedrington vers libre exercise—a very libre one indeed—is this: "OK but simply broken prose." Did this make an impression on Bill? Or did it reinforce an attitude he was already forming on his own? One way or the other, he was certainly no friend to "broken prose" later on; the study of meter—not necessarily regular meter, but emphatically meter all the same—wasn't far short of an obsession with him and formed the subject of a good many late-night conversations. A paper on the subject he wrote for one of his courses shows both an analytic capacity and a degree of sensibility that one doesn't often encounter in undergraduates—or postgraduates or, for that matter, professors.

In the same vein, SMH comments on another piece—at uncharacteristic length, and, let's candidly admit, with an uncharacteristic slight touch of pomposity—"I think you ought to begin working with the discipline of regular pattern. Young contemporary poets of stature are trying to mesh new imagery with traditional patterns." Here again, either SMH persuaded him or this resonated with an inclination already present. Bill wasn't exactly a suggestible person, but he did in fact undertake to do something not too far from what she proposed, as a glance through the work in this book will show.

One very tart observation runs: "OK if you like this sort of Beat in the Ginsberg style. I don't." The poem in question certainly isn't a very prepossessing example of the mode, and if Bill had had any inclinations in this direction, we all owe SMH a vote of thanks for steering him elsewhere.

∼

B ill graduated with honors from Pius XI and moved on to New College, in Sarasota, Florida. This milieu may require a bit of introduction in its own right.

Our college was founded in the early sixties, a time of optimism and aspiration. A fair amount of optimism would have been required; Sarasota, in those days, was a place out of Chekhov by Conrad. In this unlikely landscape of mangroves and mosquitoes a small community of émigrés from the northern snows kept the flame of Culture burning. These high-minded exiles produced plays, painted, carved and modeled, fiddled and sang, and potted and knotted to a fare-thee-well; their houses were dripping with macramé, and you couldn't take a step without bumping into some piece of chunky homemade ceramic.

Now, every Athens needs a grove of Academe, where venerable sages can stroll in sweet communion with admiring youth. And so our college was born. The slightly generic but perfectly accurate name of New College was a placeholder until some Maecenas should come along and give us enough money to take his name. Traditional approaches to education were ditched wholesale, but very high standards were nevertheless intended to be hewn to.

So far, a gentle comedy of cultural ambition. Now for the shadows in the picture: these aficionados of the Higher Things were conducting their noble experiment in the midst of a howling wilderness of crackerism. Florida was very much a southern state in those days before American society had reached its present advanced degree of homogenization. Civic and political Sarasota—the Sarasota of the courthouse and the police station—were as un-Athenian as a town could be; even to say that they were Boeotian doesn't quite do justice to the slow, slitty-eyed, simmering resentfulness and suspicion that lay over the land like a fog of poison gas as soon as you got half a mile from the beach. Thracian? Sarmatian? Pontine? I wonder whether the classical world had anything to offer resembling a small southern town in those last years of the Jim Crow regime.

Oh, well, Town and Gown are never quite happy with each other. But worse, or better, was to come when the deluge of cultural upheaval that we call the sixties swept into this already charged setting. Some of the earnest and high-minded joined the armies of psychedelia; others clung to the banner of Standards and, with horror, watched themselves morph into conservatives. Imagine a well-meaning, sensitive individual who contracts lycanthropy: he sees the hair sprouting on his palms, feels the fangs pushing between his lips, and realizes, with a sinking heart, that within minutes he will be baying at the moon.

Perhaps the defining moment came when a group of undergraduates took off for an "independent study project" that consisted of living for three weeks in tents and lean-tos on a then-desert island in the Gulf. The undertaking was duly blessed by one of the more with-it faculty, who acted as adviser, and it was also duly damned by a prominent loup-garou as a "bare-ass pot party." The independent studiers did in fact spend a lot of time in the condition alluded to, though their adviser probably missed this part of the fun. They came to be known as the "new barbarians," and whether or not they themselves coined the phrase, they adopted it as a badge of honor.

New barbarians and newly minted reactionaries were united in one thing: fear of the Yahoos at the gate. No matter how ululant and bushy-tailed the werewolves of the academic Vendée might be, there is still a great gulf fixed between egghead and redneck—the more so since some of the defenders of Standards confined their scrupulosity to the intellectual realm and lived personal lives that would embarrass a rutting mink. And of course the weed-smokers and acid-droppers lived in a permanent state of high paranoia about imminent "busts," raids, and other potential brandishments of the peckerwood nightstick. At night the dark, rustling swamps and bayous beyond the campus lights seemed terribly sinister, like a coarsely colorized print of *Cape Fear.*

Some people had a very bad time in these treacherous and uncharted waters, but others had a very good time. I think Bill was one of the latter. He had an internal compass that kept him from being swept away; but the general turmoil and up-for-grabness of everything in the culture created openings for him that might not otherwise have been available. He had no allegiance to conventional mores or attitudes, and so he got along fine with the denizens of psychedelia—after some initial reluctance; one friend tells of Bill insisting that they leave an apartment where they had planned to stay, on one of the road trips that Bill loved so much, when he found that other people there were smoking a controlled substance. This inhibition was later overcome, but his seriousness—we might even say conscientiousness—remained. He had some work he wanted to do, and some questions he wanted to answer, and slogans and song lyrics didn't satisfy him. In his travels through psychedelia, Milton and Donne and Melville and the old boy who gave us Beowulf stayed with him. Even the alpha wolves of the Standards pack thought well of Bill, because he too took the *auctores* seriously.

His capacity to get what he needed from both sides is clear from the subject matter of his work and also, I think, from its style. *Pace* SMH and her remark about "young poets of stature," Bill found a voice that was very much his own, and somewhat at variance with the prevailing taste. A note in Bill's file from the then highly regarded Robert Bly pretty much sums it up: "*The Voices* is pretty bad—it's murdered by all the archaic and 'poetic' diction—'O they call' etc, 'untracked by suppliants'—stop writing like Frankenstein's 18th century night-walker!"

But right or wrong, Bill's sense of connection with the long English lyric tradition was something he consciously clung to, and throughout his writing career he was unabashedly willing to talk about whatever old poet he happened to be learning from at the time.

Bill's attitude toward the tradition, though far from slavish, was a little unusual. Americans in general are cursed by the belief, explicit or not, that history ended not long ago and everything will be different now. Bill certainly, and not wrongly, had the sense of recent and ongoing cataclysm; his notes are full of references to the death of God, the loss of myth, and the disgroundedness of values. But at the same time he felt that he was part of an ongoing story.

A poem draft, date uncertain:

Five hundred years will stare this English down—
When New York is "an ancient town"
Yeats will be footnoted like Shakespeare,
Shakespeare as contorted as Chaucer,
And Chaucer—"one of those early English writers."
The sky's cold eye intimidates all tongues
All songs will be translated before sung,
And what's the singing if in foreign words?

More with-it writers reproached him for being "rhetorical." Bill had some thoughts of his own about rhetoric which would have seemed quite up-to-date in critical circles a few years later. In one of his random jottings, he writes: "The first thing to remember is that tropes and figures are no more rhetoric than hood ornaments are automobiles. Rhetoric has a rather bad name in the 20th century, so much so that whenever we use the term in a context of praise, we must insist that there *is* a good kind of rhetoric. Yet what we dismiss as mere rhetoric is only what every good rhetorician would likewise dismiss, since it is . . . failed rhetoric, bad rhetoric. To see the powerful uses to which rhetoric can be put, we need only look at Shakespeare, who without rhetoric would be like a body without protein."

Elsewhere, he notes, "One should use other writers as the Shake did—to remold their half-completed attempts. One should take boldly of the past, tones especially."

Bill liked poetry that had a clear prosodic structure and a clear rhetorical structure; this taste may well have been connected with his analytical side, the side that might have made him a scientist or an engineer. He also liked poems to have an argument, to be about something. In a letter written shortly after he graduated from college, he says of Dylan Thomas, "It's so exhausting, so much noise and no real toughness of thought to give it rigor. It seems mostly like a source book of great images for other people to draw on, resonant but directionless."

My own memories of Bill, on the literary side of things, are rather fragmentary, apart from the poems themselves. We didn't argue much; our attitudes and tastes were fairly similar. I do recall once a hammer-and-tongs discussion about Milton, who was not high on Bill's list at the time. I at least got him to admit that "In adamantine chains and penal fire" was a pretty good line. Bill knew Old English poetry only in modern versions, and I remember going over a big chunk of something—*The Battle of Maldon*, maybe?—word by word and explaining the syntax. He always wanted to know what poetry in other languages sounded like, and I did my thick-tongued best to oblige. The principles of Old English prosody were particularly interesting to him, and a couple of the poems in this book represent explorations in this area.

On one occasion we both went up the road to St. Petersburg for a "poetry festival" at the university there. I hitched a ride on Bill's motorcycle and have never been so terrified in my life. There was an extremely high bridge spanning the entrance to Tampa Bay, paved with open metal mesh to save weight, and Bill went hurtling over it leadfoot, as was his wont. That mesh offers no traction at all, and the crosswinds up there were wicked; on the way back, I insisted on the longer sea-level route, and Bill accommodated this wuss-out with benign good humor.

At the festival itself we had a high old time with the various schools of poetry represented. I well recall one extremely embarrassing effort by a young woman who started with the conceit of "grave = vulva" and ran with it into regions of rather overelaborate anatomical euphuism; the grass around the edge of the grave was like pubic hair, and so on—you don't want to hear the rest, believe me. Bill's face during the reading of this poem—which seemed to go on for about an hour—was a study. Normally he had a pretty good deadpan, but it failed him on this occasion. Once we escaped from the room, he dashed off a parody of the poem, which had us howling in our cups that evening to a degree that was probably rather wearisome for everybody within earshot.

It's these recollections of palship, for lack of a better word, that come more vividly to mind than any literary exchanges. Bill was a first-class pal. His excellent ear extended to this realm; he really never got it wrong. There was the right amount of competitiveness and acerbity; he never erred on the side of chumminess or overfamiliarity. But at the same time, all his pals, I'm sure, had the unspoken sense that they and Bill were fighting the same corner.

One pal recalls: "On at least one occasion, his friendship had a very direct and momentous impact on me. It was one of those partying evenings and for some reason neither of us had anything better to do than circulate from booze-up to booze-up in convoy. During the course of this evening, Bill's radar picked up the fact that a fellow student,

[Carol], was, as Bill put it, 'hunting,' and he said that he thought she had an eye for me. A little later on, he proposed that a few of us—including [Carol] and me—scale the fence to the college pool and go for a cooling dip. The suggestion was acclaimed, the dip duly taken, and [Carol] and I ended up an item, as the gossip columns say. Our relationship lasted past college for a couple of years, and then we parted. But our time together was pivotal for me; and I have Bill to thank for it."

～

Bill as matchmaker is a little uncharacteristic, but not necessarily surprising. All the dimensions of the man-woman nexus were immensely interesting to him, and he was very much a participant as well as an observer. Bill liked women a good deal, and lots of women liked him—another trait much envied by his circle of male friends. This is a slightly difficult subject to talk about. The women's movement was just getting well under way when Bill died, and his attitudes, and ours, were not exemplary by contemporary standards.

I don't mean to say that he was in any sense a misogynist. In those days one frequently heard men express some rather hateful attitudes toward women, sometimes in a jocular disguise and sometimes without bothering with any disguise. Bill never took this tone. Of course we all talked about women all the time, and Bill wasn't behindhand. But as I look back on it, what I remember was that his note was nearly always a note of admiration for something, if only the curve of somebody's lip or the texture of her skin. This is not to say that he was incapable of joking on the subject.

One member of Bill's circle recalls an occasion, highly characteristic of the time and the place, when a dining-room discussion turned to possible etymologies for the word "poontang." The relish of this conversation may have been heightened by the fact that a faculty member, not universally beloved, had brought his wife to sample the glutinous college food that evening, and the couple were seated at an adjoining table. Bill, after listening for some time with his slightly owlish, bemused expression, piped up with the "archaic" form "Pwan Twan," meaning "place of great rest." This bit of fictive scholarship was delivered in the tone of donnish solemnity that Housman might have used to propose an emendation of Aeschylus. It was this line that finally sent the slumming faculty pair home—without their dessert, one hopes, remembering the level of New College cuisine.

In a rather odd way, though, Bill was chivalrous. Chivalry, of course, is as disreputable as misogyny; but candor obliges me to record the fact. Bill did not talk about his "conquests," much less brag about them. He could have talked about them a good deal, because they were many.

Like most men in those days, he tended to divide the world of women into two groups: the ones you worshipped and the ones from whom you sought . . . comfort, shall we say. His choice of worship objects was no more infallible than anybody else's. In spite of his own mastery of the Enigmatic Mode, Bill was as big a sucker as the next guy for the remote, cool, inaccessible Artemis type, and he occasionally found himself languishing on the banks of some still water that really didn't run very deep at all.

But in spite of their less exalted position in the Hedrington hierarchy, the comforters are (to my taste) perhaps the more interesting group. Accomplished, successful, capable women now, with children (and, sometimes, husbands, when a tolerable one can be found); women with well-paid jobs and published books; women respected and sometimes feared by their colleagues and underlings; women who are not, in short, wearing a "kick me" sign: this is how the graduates of Bill's College of Comforters have tended to turn out.

In talking about Bill now, the former transient girlfriends still speak of him, usually, with kindness and affection, and some degree of puzzlement. They too, in spite of their intimacy with Bill, found it difficult to read him and sometimes still wonder just what the relationship was about. It seems that he made no hypocritical claims of devotion, but neither was he cold or unkind. If he was using them, in what would now be considered a somewhat deplorable way, he didn't rub their noses in the fact.

"We developed an odd relationship," writes one alumna, "not in frequent contact, but spending time together in unplanned ways. I felt myself to be a supportive friend, and then of course we were also occasional lovers. Bill had a reserve about relationships, and for all I know the times we shared a bed may have been only meeting a physical need, not an emotional one. That was not a question I asked."

Another says, "He was interesting and didn't condescend to me (which was terribly important to me then . . . it was my own babe peri-

24

od). It was also natural, given the mores of the place, that we would become lovers.

"Sadly, I cannot remember any of the details. . . . And this is extremely odd and terribly distressing. I have not one brightly lit scene of us as lovers. . . . The two clear memories I do have are of his wandering silhouette on the nighttime campus and a motorcycle ride we took, near the end of our relationship.

"I do know what attracted me, and it was not simply that I was lonely and he was available. I think that what we all want from love is to know and be deeply known. And Bill was very, very good at this, or at least played it very well. It was part of his poet persona, you see. The sensitive writer, the close observer of nature and human nature. This was a killer attraction when combined with the forceful motorcycle delinquent, the devil-take-our-cares thrill seeker. He listened to me as if I were the most fascinating person he had ever encountered. He noticed small details. He paid attention. This is quite irresistible to most women, and was to me.

"I think now that I was fooled by him, and that is why I have no explicit memories. I think that he was seeing me as a writer first and a lover second. . . . he didn't do much revealing of his own, except through the writing."

The same correspondent records an instance of Bill's style of chivalry. A contretemps with another boyfriend had left her isolated from her circle of friends, who apparently took the boyfriend's side. During this period in Coventry, she writes: "I went to [a] party alone, talked to some other, peripheral folks, wandered awkwardly, felt like crying and running away. Just then, Bill strode into the room like the dark knight he fancied himself. My hero! My rescuer! Nobody knew that we were lovers. . . . At that moment the spotlight was on Hedrington. He came over, all casual and cool cowboy dude, took my hand, leaned down and asked if I wanted to split. Did I? You bet! I will always be grateful to him for just that one perfect, gallant and empathic gesture."

≈

Writer first, lover second just about gets the range. Bill wasn't unsympathetic—quite the contrary. But the notes he wrote to himself about the life going on around him suggest that his restless intelligence, his desire to figure out things and people, was greatly in the ascendant.

These notes are not cold, but they are uncomfortably clear-sighted. He is often puzzled or bemused but never seems to be much confused by identification, projection, wishful thinking, or envy—by his own needs, in short. Though the notes are often about what he is thinking, they are very seldom about him. He shows little or no trace of the adolescent's love affair with the mirror. He is as elusive in his diary as he is in his poems; but as with the poems, the world around him is keenly observed and deeply pondered. He enters into the lives of others with imaginative sympathy but quite without sentimentality. One of his casually scribbled aphorisms, apropos of nothing obvious, sets the tone: "Remember, mercy must be tempered with justice."

An early example of Bill the high-school social observer: "I'm just writing this tonight cuz these people are so funny. There is one whose mother committed suicide and one who is fixated on his sister, one who knows his father hates him—then there is the one who is what is known as a 'closet-case', a homosexual who won't admit it to himself. There are the lonely girls and the involuted boys, the boy who is on an endless round of meaningless sex, the boy who has a life expectancy of 10 years max if he smokes, which he does, the boy who was drunk for 3 months straight last year, the boy who has twisted a certain girl and the girl who can't let go of him and writes endless poems about him." "Funny," he says. But he doesn't really seem to be laughing: just taking it all in.

Another unrelenting observation: "[Ann] has white narrow pinched face with tight lips and light laughter—straight hair ending in mid neck, but after love she is pink & smooth & relaxed & happy & full." The same girl appears often: "After months [Ann] is so afraid of me that she fears to talk—long periods of silence precede her speeches—she is astonished that anybody could want her so much." The same entry continues, "[Ben] has been hurt terribly by girls, I think. Frankie by the Old Drunk—to twist someone like that is hell."

More from the Milwaukee year: "When we are together I think of all the people doing the same in a thousand Milwaukee parlors and of the (cordage of my fathers) ancestors who have lived and died to let us be one; I am grafted on to you." The phrase "cordage of my fathers" refers to early drafts of the poem that became "for my father."

His gimlet eye does extend to himself on occasion: "I have heard it said that poets put salt on their wounds so that they can feel their experiences more sharply. I think not. I think it is lye."

Or again (this, once more, from high school): "Standing on the street with [Charlie, Dave, and Ann]—oscillating between them uncertain of who to stand by. Talking to exec on stairs feeling superior to what he said but humbled in my work clothes." As with many of his notes, the point here seems to be: how interesting that one can feel this way. Any adolescent might have recorded such feelings, but few would have done so in quite such an analytical tone.

Occasional Hamlet-like "my tables!" memoranda-to-self occur: "You really have to defend yourself against your own conscience or superego for it will attack you with religion, morality, custom, anything—other people use it also to control you so be on the lookout."

One page of tedious class notes has later been pressed into service for a wild series of disconnected scribbles, fueled, one suspects, by the fumes of *Cannabis sativa*. A dry little comment, penned in a corner of this farrago, observes, "This use of this paper has made the class notes immortal." So this is Bill, high as the proverbial kite, anticipating me, reading him observing himself. . . . Well, enough of *that*.

In addition to these random jottings, he also kept a more systematic journal, though as with most such undertakings, the entries become less frequent over time. Its first page, from October 1967, his second year at New College, reads, in part: "I am concerned with [Beth]—she is exceptional and the other pillowheads fade beside her—She said I was ugly—I don't think she could take the truth about [Ed] & me & older students & 1st year students & her. Perhaps, like art, life needs some indirection. . . . Anyhow, I made a mistake and must now pay for it alone. . . . I am very tired . . . perhaps I'll chase a pillowhead just to give me what ease a person like that can. . . . I'd like to give something to [Ed & Beth] but I don't know what—my absence perhaps."

Most of the book, though, concerns itself more with what he was thinking than with his social life. A later entry from the same year reflects on his own intellectual evolution: "It is strange that I was drawn to poetry—2 years ago I was so analytical—my interpretations of experience were demythologized except for conventional myths. . . . Science can point to things & make ideal models (which of course are a kind of myth too) but it cannot give the slightest value."

The social sciences take a few lumps too: "A history book is like a stone thrown into the darkness of a huge echo chamber in order to silence a barking dog."

His own aspirations are recorded unblushingly: "So many people make radical declarations & take radical stands when young, only to back down later—one thing I want is to so identify with my role. . . . that I can never escape at some future date into the kind of life Mr. [F.] chose. I want to become a truth teller."

Occasionally there are expressions that suggest an almost hallucinatory vividness of perception, even when chemical assistance doesn't appear to be involved. There are several references to the "Isness of the napkin holder in the snack bar," though this epiphany is not discussed in detail. Bill alludes, in the same context, to "the radical contingency of [Professor J.]'s arm," and there are enigmatic references to "Unspeakable Thoughts"—those are Bill's capitals—which come to him on occasion. And once he says, with a rather startling matter-of-factness, "Am going into the Fear today—have been close to it for a week to 10 days."

A lengthy entry records some reading in thermodynamics and information theory, topics which became and remained quite important to Bill. The connection between information and entropy was one that he found richly suggestive. He seems to have found a link between these ideas and his quest for a new basis for values and what he called "Myth," the old ones having notoriously dropped the ball, as far as Bill and much of our generation were concerned.

"It's been fun breaking the rules," he writes, "Yes, very much fun, but what now? Perhaps without the rules there's no game. . . . Today we have, as usual, our particular combination of reason & unreason. We use the vestige of the enlightenment to attack codes of morality as insupportable by any scientific data—then proceeded to act totally emotionally about the effects of the disintegration. . . . Perhaps I've been reasonable too long and now it's time to be unreasonable. If people don't artificially limit their experience by systems or contracts with reality, everything can and does happen. . . . How much chaos can we take—the Word really creates."

For a literary guy, he seldom makes specifically literary comments; he's more inclined to relate his reading to his big questions of Value and Myth. But every so often an obiter dictum whizzes past: "Poetically speaking, *Murder in the Cathedral* is on about the same level as *Gammer Gurton's Needle.*" The comparison is unfair to the Gammer, but not bad.

~

The late sixties were not all fun and games, of course. There was a war on, and we were all keenly aware of it; it makes an appearance in some of the poems in this book. Like most of us, Bill was determined not to participate. He wasn't a particularly political guy—I don't ever remember having a political conversation with him—but he shared the general, somewhat diffuse, attitude of resistance to authority in general and skepticism about patriotic slogans that prevailed in our milieu.

His family was completely behind him. Frank Newton, who served in Korea, was characteristically definite: "I figured if you really didn't believe in it you shouldn't go—I know some of these Vietnam veterans would rip my head off for saying that. I figured he'd taken steps to stay out of it. Didn't bother me none."

It's not clear exactly how he did manage to "stay out of it." He did get a notice to report for his physical. And in his paper trove are copies of two letters, written to his draft board, by dean of students Arthur MacArthur Miller and campus chaplain Horace Cooper. These make interesting, evocative reading nowadays.

Arthur Miller's letter has a very suspicious flavor of near parody. Was this intentional, or was he just laying it on a little thick? "The written report of William's most recent diagnostic session confirms my long-standing suspicion of this student's erratic behavior. . . . His use of dangerous and unprescribed drugs, including those much stronger than cannabis, has aggravated his problems. This college cannot tolerate such abuse of drugs."

Oh, Mac, I think, as I read this, aren't we a bit close to the wind now? Isn't your nose growing? He continues, in the same fulminant vein: "William has certain pronounced and peculiar qualities of mind which have carried him through a loosely structured college program. . . . Speaking myself as an Army officer (Cpt. USAR) and a current military instructor . . . I cannot imagine William as a present credit to the service. . . . As [his] pattern of drug abuse is likely to continue after leaving college, I frankly cannot hope that his mental health is likely to improve."

Horace Cooper's letter strikes a less Blimpish note, but equally accentuates the negative: "I have known [Bill] for almost three years and have a considerable degree of personal intimacy with him. Last year . . . he took [psychological tests] which indicated serious emotional and psychic dysfunctions. . . . [his] 'highest' scores were those which revealed Anxiety-Tension-Stress and Inadequacy in feelings and behavior. He also scored significantly in the Compulsive-Obsessive-Rigid Behavior group and in Motivation-Goals. Mr. Hedrington and I had a discussion of these matters, in which he disclosed that his difficulties were of long standing and he felt he had not made much progress in resolving them.... In view of the above, I cannot believe he will function adequately in the military environment, with which I have had much experience [as a chaplain in the air force]."

Bill's draft board was the Sarasota one, rather than one back home in Wisconsin. Knowing the type of people who ran Sarasota in those days, and the antagonism that many of them felt towards the "hippies" of New College, it seems mildly surprising that letters like these should have done the trick. On the other hand, the Sarasota draft board had other pools of young men to draw from; perhaps they just decided that it wasn't worth pursuing somebody who had the motivation and the support to put up a struggle. In any case, Bill was spared the choice between Vietnam and Canada.

∼

Bill and I graduated from New College at the same time, the spring of 1970. He went to take up a one-year creative writing fellowship at Stanford, and I to the dungeons of graduate school in Chicago.

By this time the entries in his journal have become very infrequent. He does write, at one point, "Dr Johnson—GREAT!" which hugely pleases me to read, because I was always talking up the great Cham to Bill at college, and he wasn't (yet) buying. He records a dream in which class takes place "underground, in a dungeon, wet, dark." He was reading "Rabelais, Winters, Blackmur, Auden crit, Stevens crit, 17th century lyric, 16th century lyric, Bradley, Age of Shakespeare, Moby Dick, *Timon of Athens,* poems of Hardy, Tate poems, Ransom crit, much Winters crit, Chaucer, *Rage For Order* (forgettable), Auerbach *Mimesis* (very good), *Axel's Castle* (good!), *Winter's Tale* (1st time), Montaigne essays, article on circuit breakers." The circuit breakers are highly characteristic.

A lengthy letter to our New College teacher Robert Knox gives more detail: "For a while now I've felt that my reading of Yeats had reached a certain impasse, unlike any I'd felt before, not that I'd exhausted him, but that after 4 years of him being my regular standby reading, I was ready for something else. So I turned to Frost. Unbelievable! There's so much going on that I didn't ever see there before. . . .

"Frost has more a complexity of tone, whereas Yeats had one of symbolism, so I've been jumping up and down at the change. What a sly old rascal that New England Delphic village seer was! . . . Part of it is that humor, that non-committal wavering between maybes. A big part tho is the dramatic aspect. How much more you can infer in a situation!

"I've been reading some books on rhetoric. I found this fine solid standby book of about 1900 called *The Working Principles of Rhetoric*. So far I've avoided any of those god-damned modern semanticaler-than-thou studies but I'll take a dip to see how the water is. . . .

"This Frost thing has really increased my ability to see how one can play with language to make it suggestive. It's like a constant subtle indirection to find direction out. . . . Frost has that same feeling for me that Yeats has, that all the poems add to the whole, that there's value in each for all. . . .

"Been reading plays—Chekhov is so much better than the rest it's incredible. . . . he knew how to infold all the edges to make it seamless. I read *Absalom, Absalom!*—it's good but it's too rhetorical Dr. Knox, some of those passages of miasmal murk embarrassed me exceeding much."

Here too, the straight-faced, burlesque-Malory note of "exceeding much" is decidedly Bill's idiom.

Bill's next destination, after Stanford, was Syracuse University, where he had landed a fellowship in the writing program. During the intervening summer, as was his habit, he roamed the country, staying a few days here and a few days there. He spent some time visiting Jane Farrier, as I'll call her here, a fellow student whose orbit had intersected with Bill's, intensely but inconclusively, at college. She writes: "My overall impression was that Bill was confident about the future, happy with his new undertaking and pleasantly distracted. As always, his deep dark side was never far from the surface. It seemed more integrated, less likely to overwhelm. That made him more playful, and willing to be more transparent emotionally. He still had an endearing touch of the Eeyore, guessing that he would be hurt in love again. . . . One of the things I miss most is his capacity for elegant understatement and gesture, especially about emotional subjects."

Bill stopped by my place in Chicago for a few days late that summer. He had given up his famous motorcycle and acquired a much-used little two-seater English sports car. It was not in great shape. The passenger-side door didn't open; one had to climb over it to get in. Bill's style of driving was perhaps somewhat improved from his college days, but not by much.

I was *solus rex* in my stifling Hyde Park apartment that summer; my then girlfriend was away, on some ultracool tropical biology expedition, and I was moping enviously around, trying to make our Salvation Army furniture look a little more presentable with sandpaper and linseed oil. Bill's visit was a godsend.

He was tactful as always. I was trying to learn to cook and one evening made some appalling mess with oxtail and bargain-basement wine, which poor Bill gamely ate. He showed me the poems he had been working on during his Stanford year. He had been working, as he said in a letter to Robert Knox, on "trying to write something longer, but still good." His New College productions had mostly been in a very compressed, ultralyrical vein, but now he was spreading his wings a bit and exploring a more narrative, discursive style; perhaps his reading of Frost had encouraged this turn. In addition to his good ear, he was a thoughtful, reflective person—no *vox et praeterea nihil*—and I thought he was doing pretty well with it. Some of these poems are in this collection.

I have a vivid image of him handing me a sheaf of manuscript and settling into a chair opposite me: "So now," he said, "I'm going to take the uneasy chair." I didn't believe it for a minute, even then. He wasn't shy about showing his stuff to people, and though he was interested in what they had to say, his internal compass was too strong for criticism to cause him much disquiet. But the compliment was well turned; Bill knew how to make himself agreeable.

He seemed happy. Calmer, more relaxed, less cautious and restrained. Still very much in control of what he said and did, but his repertoire in every sense had expanded. I wish now I could remember more of what we talked about during that time. I do recall that I was sorry to see him go, notwithstanding the old saw about fish and houseguests.

It was the last time I saw him or heard from him. There is one final entry in his journal: "October 29, 1971. 209 Comstock [his apartment in Syracuse]. Chinese, 3 a.m. [Jane] is in [another state]. Idled all summer to no good end except some good time at Frank's.

"I am in some ways much more settled than I was in Sarasota. I feel very drawn to a sense of commonality with other people. Tho I get unhappy my mind plays few jumping tricks. I have a sense of implicit order, as in a Bach concerto. Tonight my mind is calm, in stasis, trying to figure out what all this is all about. Very attracted to Bible, to true things which can help us to live. Borges and Barth now seem odd to me. I don't know if it's good or not that this is happening. Aristotle's *Poetics* is very good."

And with those words, Bill signs off from the world of our knowing. Two days later he was dead. The details are unclear; he was driving his little convertible along a Syracuse highway, fast as usual, with another grad student, Cenan Ozgurel, the son of a Turkish diplomat. Somehow he lost control of the car and "sideswiped a telephone pole," according to a report in a local newspaper. The car flipped over and both Bill and Ozgurel were killed instantly.

The news came to us, in Chicago, on the dark evening of November 1: All Hallows' Day, when Christendom once saw itself enfolded by the great assembly of those who have gone before; and earlier still, the immemorial solemnity of Samhain, when old Celtic Europe propitiated the even older dead, those vanished builders of henge and barrow, tumulus and menhir. I can't recall exactly how we heard that Bill had been killed. What I can recall was the robotic numbness with which we reacted. There were, for some reason, several other ex–New College people there; and for some time we went about our business, whatever it was, with a kind of catatonic indifference. Finally somebody figured out that we ought to go to the funeral. And so we did; six or seven of us all jammed into a car, for the long drive north and west to Chippewa Falls.

A strange sight we must have made when we got there. We were all trying to be respectable, but our wardrobe of jackets and ties and little black dresses left much to be desired, after the deluge of the sixties. Our hair was long and shaggy, and beards abounded. We piled out of the car, after driving through the night, in front of St. Charles Church, and somehow or other—I remember none of this—made ourselves known to Bill's family.

Robert Knox had suggested that one of us should ask to read a poem at the funeral—it was Stephen Spender's "I think continually of those who were truly great"—and this was, very generously, allowed. I don't remember the church, I don't remember the coffin. I remember walking to the chancel steps and reading the poem, and I remember that my throat felt like some mechanism made of brass producing words without my participation. Not that there was anything wrong with the words:

"the soul's history"; "endless and singing." The brazen mechanism began to show signs of malfunction. It finally broke down on the phrase "grave evening demand for love." Temporary repairs were effected; but by the end I was reduced to something not much better than barking. "Left the vivid air signed with their honor." The growl of that final 'r' sounded like an electric drill in the echoing church and seemed to hang in the air forever.

The priest spoke, of course. He hadn't known Bill. This sort of thing can't be easy. He was very struck by the fact that this improbable carload of odd-looking young folks had driven all that way to be present, and his homily ended up turning on that: Bill must have been quite a guy, if. ...We were all deeply embarrassed and thought it was horribly lame and inadequate.

Well, of course it was inadequate. Funeral speeches, I have since discovered, always are. But maybe the good father was onto something. Even in the bare bones of Bill's life story, there's a pattern that comes strongly out: Bill, literally from his cradle, somehow brought to his side a new mother and father, a new brother and sister, and in later years rallied helpers, allies, teachers, sponsors, protectors, comforters, and mourners. Nor has this gift failed him even now, when he has been dust for three decades: here we are, all present and sober, an editor and publisher—and there *you* are, I hope, his readers. He drew people to him like a lodestone, and they embraced his cause and made it their own. Bill himself, in himself, was a mystery. Rummaging through his papers, talking with his family, and looking at old photos brings him back vividly but does not illuminate the enigma. There is, at last, nothing better to tell you, posterity, who didn't know him, than this: the guy was *irresistible.*

∼

After all his restless roaming, Bill lies at last in Prairie View Cemetery, outside the town where he grew up. As you drive in, a large sign at the cemetery entrance promises "perpetual care." Perpetuity is a long time, but the promise has been kept—so far, anyway. The grounds are tidy, the grass green and mowed like a Marine's haircut. But the name is less than candid. There's no prairie in sight; the vistas from Bill's corner are a tank farm to the south and a humming highway to the west. Next to Bill are Earl and Clara, whose headstones call them "Mother" and "Father." Bill's own says "Son." Bill's stone also bears the inscription "The Lord is my shepherd." This jars a bit: not what he would have chosen, surely. On the other hand, it is from a poem. Better, as usual, in the original. The word we translate as "shepherd" is actually a verb form: "God is the one who is herding me." This is the sort of thing Bill would have liked to know. Centuries of piety have blurred the startling character of the image. From the sheep's point of view, the shepherd's motives are obscure at best, and certainly not identical with the sheep's conception of his interests. And the shepherd has a dog, whose attentions have no obviously benign character. Bill's puzzlement at just where and why we are being herded did full justice to the inscrutability of our predicament. And he had, it seems, his own Black Dog nipping at his heels. No doubt his fleece was all the thicker as a result, but is this a trade-off that anybody would choose?

Everybody knows how the poem continues. If we can clear away the Sunday school associations, it's not such a bad fit, really. Bill, as we have seen, evoked something in people, and never lacked for helpers, guardians, and good angels. The green pastures, the still waters, and so on, were all in fact provided—though there were plenty of rugged and rocky passages, too, in Bill's grazing grounds.

He is done now with verdant land and dry. The lush lawns of Prairie View are nothing to him, and the perpetual care he requires is not the kind a groundskeeper can give. He is in your hands, O unknown and unimaginable posterity, in his book; a book far too thin, but undeniably and strongly full, full to overflowing, with the strange richness and rich strangeness of an infinitely remarkable life.

On the Downhill Side

The Voices

I was born on the downhill side,
late in the year, in early December,
in the light's heavy dip and hesitation,
when the old peoples prayed for beginning
in the snow-salted fields
and scattered bitterness of corn stalks;
but though I came fatly of that gaunt race,
though it was a different end and today that day,
the fields untracked by supplicants,
the corncribs many, and full,
still I carry their disappointed dead
buried in my body,
and am the outspoken child
of the silent generations of my cells—
for O, they call with the old voices,
in a millennium length of words,
in the thousand year cries of the dead,
that their lean voices, lost to these fields,
may be gathered up and justified in me.

Apple

The dead litter so,
leave clothes in drawers,
old photographs, everything,
and go.

They are as thoughtless as children,
who will get up with the sun,
take an apple,
and set out for the world's end.

Gone

Even after the goodbye kiss
there was the waiting
for the walk to the plane and waving,
there was the drawing up of steps
and doors closing,
the taking off,
and still the requisite tedium of disappearing:
always a raveling dress
caught on a cabinet knob,
always in her "coiffure" a hair
from the back of nowhere just hanging;
there is even her handbag after the plane's gone.

Near-accident

The wheels spun instants,
but the whole car was hours
in the arriving, arriving, arriving,
its massive, death-making power
awesome in its actual density,
the important, indifferent driver
fascinated out his left window by flowers,
but I jumped back, alive!
I've been lightweight in life ever since.

Water

Her rhythm is the measured walk
a half-step from a skip;
her time an hour distant,
until the smiling instant!

O would that she were what she seems,
or would seem whatever she is,
for I can forget the shape of ice,
but go mad remembering water.

Glass

The glass tension releasing he knelt down
on pain to free himself among the bits,
and crooning at the smoothness of the glass,
caressed his wrist to calm himself and rest.

But bandages and tape bound back the blood,
and the tile was cleansed, and nothing was left
to tell the sometime deep demand for glass
to break the frail containment of the skin.

Lest You Believe Walt ...

In the gravid trees' hydraulic green,
Buds breeding-hard under the grown load,
When the earth's belly swells big to bleed,
And the mud labors, and the seeds groan,
Even Bambi has humped, even the white-tail deer
Have taken their tails down off the knoll,
The does staggering heavy and sweating to kneel
And fall thickly in the bracken at Spring's door.

On Hearing Freshmen Argue About the Existence of God

And thus it is the first year here; the one
Female, Catholic, certain—St. Thomas sent
To prove the fact of God by argument.
Her "infinite regression" is welldone.
The other though, semantic, male, and done
With God, proves proof of the omnipotent
Is sermon, and that what she thought she meant
Is meaningless, and at best emotion.
God, Anne, come here, and we will argue too,
And set the Spirit at the null and void—
We've done it once and know more than they do
Of point and counterpoint—how to avoid
The question—how to attack—and when through,
Of what to do when both sides are destroyed.

On Deck

The fist that punched the pasteboard mask
Pulls back; and Ahab's lost a leg.
And should he dare disturb the universe,
Or even care? The child who plays at mumbly-peg
Enjoys his two fat legs—no worse
For idleness or innocence.
Is Ahab's madness loss of sense,
Or should he cock his fist a second time,
And ask whatever question there's to ask,
Or should he hunt the narwhale and the right?
On deck! man Ahab harpoons Prime,
White water downs the Pequod, White
Heals the sea of pride; the child plays; the mask
That Ahab dies at watches both do each his task.

Like Quakers

Unless I take like Quakers thees and thous,
And break this bucking English into rhyme,
How will I tell you that which only vows
Exceed, because they recognize no time?
My good-enough, everyday, bronco tongue,
As everybody knows, will do for day;
High-talking's hard on a work-a-day lung,
That has to eat the dirt man eats for pay.
But after nightfall, when the day slows down,
I'll study Greek and Latin rhetorick,
While you take off your cotton dress, and gown
Yourself in bedsheets, and each night I'll pick
Some new old Roman speech to hobble me,
For else I'd naught but babble love to thee.

The Others

My others are the thousand shallow breaths
A man will take to give himself short sleep,
Safe by minor lives in minor deaths,
And warm where water will not tell the deep
Tall mountains of the central sea, or read
The hard high-pressure country of its floor,
But only wets the night it can't exceed,
And proves with less how much I need the more,
But my one with you is like the deep-drawn air
That pins the lungs, like the mile-under dark
Of the Atlantic, and the river there
That sweeps a quarter earth in one salt arc
And never tires; but I, tiring, again
Will rest myself with others, until when.

The Boats

The boats that bump so docile at the dock
Are moored there slackly; no rowboat captain
Even, but knows the moon-called sea takes line,
And will have it, or hang the boats to break.
I'm not a boat, my will is not a rope,
And you, for all your changes and your pull
tiding my heart's rerunning salty well,
Are not the pumicestone that queens the deep.
Yet, I might as well be boat, and you moon,
For though I fight, my blood bends with the sea,
My body aching at my twisted will.
How, unless a man tie back the ocean,
Can taut lines help but snap, and how, once free,
Can any man but be a tide-bound hull?

Shutdown

Death shut down the works, the factory's old.
The union of the dead has won, and quit.
Will his eyes be opened by the cold?

The economy is strong, the market bold,
The people as a whole are not hard hit.
Death shut down the works, the factory's old.

The management holds on, when it can hold—
Tonight the doctor packs his useless kit.
Will his eyes be opened by the cold?

What a question—it's common—factories fold;
Dark windows only show the soul is lit.
Death shut down the works. The factory's old.

Yet whatever reassuring story's told,
The after silence mocks the telling it:
Will his eyes be opened by the cold?

By his works, would that faith, like dreams, were sold—
A man must be a scab! Do not admit
Death, shutdown—the work's, the factory's old;
Will his eyes! Be opened by the cold!

Knowing the Time

When the last
local point of interest
has been marveled over,
and the folder
of "Things to See and Do"
is shut in a drawer,
and Mom and Dad are finally
settled for good
with their own kind,
they start to always
know what time it is,
without looking almost,
like children out of school
who play school
to shorten summer;
and tired of always knowing
almost without looking,
they retire to local bars,
crowding in the cocktail hours
to drink at special rates
the Senior Citizens' Special,
the newcomers chatting
of children and grandchildren,
regulars quiet mostly,
mostly watching themselves
in the mirror watching
behind the bottles
behind the bar,
until they drink up where
no one ever
knows the time.

Old Women at the Check-out Counter

They are afraid, of course: boots and helmet
mean motorcycle, mean young—and alien;
so they pick and pull at their worn sweaters,
and rustle among themselves of T.V. shows,
the high price of lunch meat on a pension,
the shuffleboard scores in their condominium.
But still they peep at me and what I've bought:
the razor blades, the metal polish, the beer.
I move to leave, having many things to do,
and now eager to do them now, but one
speaks up to me and stops me, wondering,
until she quavers out "You forgot your stamps."—
her arm jerking randomly—"They're good to save."
I leave them as some kind of gift and leave.

Locked In

The car splayed wide the gray stone wall
in abrupt stop;
as leisurely as July,
the door swung back and slammed;
dust went humming in the sun.
Blood soon stopped,
but other things went on—
the stones began to settle in the grass,
the left rear tire sighed flat;
a panting farmer jumped the wall and pulled,
and pulled at the bent door, and quit:
the angle of the head was plain,
the driver was locked in.
His day-long labor lost, with nothing to do,
he waited out his gasping,
until, as silent as the other one,
he moved his legs and left,
perhaps beginning to be afraid
there are not doors enough to get outside.

Deliverance

I have delivered her to madness
And am quiet now.
The chair remains a chair;
I must remember that
I am quiet now.
The coiling, flicking of its arms
Is not there.
What she saw
Is not there.
The breath may lie, and the mind believe;
I speak with an urgent breath
To myself.
I have delivered her
And will not talk with her.
Though she speaks in a voice beyond lies
And shrieks in the last vision;
I will remain quiet
About the chair
And ignore her.
I cannot help her.
I will remain quiet
And the chair will remain quiet.

Bicycling Away from the Library

Rosewater and dust the dawn;
whir and grit of tires,
grumble of gear and chain
and the fine rain
nerve-white along the skin
as the round webs turn
their long miles down the day . . .
push and push, right and left,
the pedals down and down
riverrun your revolution
downstream drift of wheel and dream
by book and magazine past paper drain
our unloosed lives in your dark run
that we may join our urgent night
allow the turning waterwheel
lost to the buzz of black and white,
that clash of opinions
a Tower of Babel and confusion of tongues.

Photographs

Click! my light caught in black and white.
Remember the Amusing Anecdote? how native blacks
broke the magic box to free their souls?
Remember how explorers laughed? If I could laugh . . .
for six hours I have hunted my soul,
scattered drawers and stripped walls,
decimated photograph albums,
keeping a small fire going,
freeing myself picture by picture:
myself at one year eating ice cream,
myself at five petting a spaniel,
at ten on a bike, fifteen a car,
brown, flare, and burn, every one, into air!
Unless I loose the light caught in these shots,
bound in a boy, I will die to my full flame
never to become my essential sun,
memory wholly burned in pure oxygen.

6 A.M.

Instantly awake and shocked tight,
in the light's smashed mountain,
broken granite and gray air,
my eyes gouged open,
my body a fear in flesh;
why snapped from sleep?
No noise did it, not the light,
not any dream in memory;
why awake?

The sudden day slips into normal calm,
the hours mass their usual ease,
and noon and afternoon are gone,
with all their small antitheses,
and the slight drag of doubt, the snag
that warps the river just a bit,
ignore it.
You may, perhaps, forget for good,
unless, of course, some morning stabs your eyes,
the gulfs and cliffs that drift by through our days.

Freefall

No one returns an All-American
from here; the first law you must learn is breathe,
the second, walk; if the language cools
enough to speak, then you swear allegiance,
as if you could care, as if a country
could naturalize such aliens.
Which of you knows this freefall of the mind,
the nausea of the weightless man, lost
out of eclipse, the burning of the Word
become its full and Pentecostal sun,
and worst, the realizing as you lose
profane faith in mere reality,
how many, and deep, are the levels of sleep.

For My Grandfather

When my grandfather went away,
October headed north into the winter,
and I was cold of the crying
in back bedrooms, restless at the whispers,
at the fussing of leaves in the mouths of the house.
Away myself from the cooling house,
from the dusting of my mother, away,
far as grandfather, who left me there,
who left with his German into the north,
away at the creek, rock-walking the granite,
I was quiet as Sunday in an autumn town,
my game strange with the haze of the burning leaves
as they lost their small summer to winter.
Even then, though my coat wore out that day,
thinner as the wind blew back from the winter,
though the water hurt as it wet the rocks,
even then I was childish and able to play,
only quiet in my stepping from rock to rock,
wishing the dusting would stop, and the whispers,
and that my grandfather were there.
Now, in the drought in the middle of winter,
one of my impermanent winters
only of weather and my gradual age,
as the sun swings down in a dead-end month,
with water dust in its dunes of snow,
twenty more years have lengthened the thought
of a playing child in smoky October.
My mother that day couldn't dust enough
to stop the burning up by breath
of all our combustible selves, but grandfather,
guttural tongue stiff with the winter,
left us seventy years when he left,
and proved by the sudden north of the house

that human fire is our first house,
and we are the waste which makes increase.

One Day at a Catholic University

The morning reconstruction done,
books fit to the category Books,
records fit to the class Records,
everything fit to Something,
and nothing slurring into anything else,
I begin by getting up.

I notice on my way to class
that I have shaved and showered
and apparently changed clothes.
I smile: habit is a priceless nurse.

Today the class is on Camus,
and while they settle Suicide,
I doodle my way through.
          When it's over I leave.

Lunch is good. The afternoon
is like falling
until I stop it.
I regulate my breathing
and continue.

Back to the window for light,
I sit,
reading the Church on Camus—
in nineteen scintillant pages,
a Jesuit concludes that "really,
the Absurd is silly."

Dinner. Tired today. The fork wouldn't work
and I had to give up.
It's early to sleep
I think I must
I undress
lie down
let it collapse.

December Aubade

You, who will shortly land
smiling in a wailing plane,
gray eyes and gray wool dress,
from the land of the blank white field
and the black upright tree;
bring some order into Florida.
A proper winter will freeze
the intricate quick water,
and make even a walk downtown
a thought-out thing.
While here the sun still burns,
the water is continual;
no stillness and too much of change.
But you promised me snow,
somehow you'd bring snow,
and if I looked quickly,
I might find in crystal
a brief symmetry,
before the sun takes even that away.
But whatever coldness you can bring,
bring some, and quickly! come!
for the long light of the morning sun
allows only my continual walking.

Flare

The compressed breath
bound in a tank of oxygen
burst into his face God's word Flare!
then nothing seeing there.

But oh, how his face took it,
ingathering all that light,
his eyes used up at once,
his features chopped to scrap,
and all of it an instant Gloria.

Then under the knives and eyes he lay,
lost and found in the light in his face,
while they . . .
picked out many bits,
left many.
Few of the attendants
thought it was worth-while.
Even as, in joy, he tried to smile,
they knew what explosion meant,
what really happened that he might not see:
an abrupt, but small,
yet permanent,
increase in entropy.

The Change to Ariel: For Sylvia Plath

Sylvia, come, come, come;
you were the only, the very woman, the one
sick enough of sunlight to take the sun;
skinning your eyes of daily lids,
your mind of caution and the Golden Mean,
you scribbled all the way one droning note,
then shed your nothing song as Ariel,
deep-breathing death's strange oxygen,
and stared forever into noon.
Were you left-handed, did you cast a shadow,
what was the clue? Now you've tuned our Sirens
who goes next, forgetting human form,
hungry to learn that manic monotone?
Ariel, I sweat and want to burn.
Teach me, woman, how you made the change.
Nothing is enough. My summer's winter sun
itself is worthless till it's off or on.

Sight

You may look. Do not stare.
If you dare
fix eyes on desk or chair,
on anything for long,
if you dare,
your sight will disappear in its mere fire,
retina burned beyond all light
by something so much there.
Boys blind, lids down to cover stones,
sit in the chairs that took their eyes,
say nothing, hold in their black brains
the image of those chairs,
say nothing, days by hours gone,
nothing, hold that frame of fire, those cells
recycling everything they finally saw,
silence their last end,
our noise our ignorance, our sight, our sin.

Acceleration

Out of the fuzz of men and mouths,
riding the sun cracked from gasoline,
twin megaphones lay down
the original red roar,
and I have my fist around fire!
Ahead world blooming with rate,
behind world dead by my speed,
twist out the last nova of wrist,
star!
grow now and breathe, slow beyond speed,
with light as my limit, my loss, my release,
where time has no name but enough.

Student Accident

A fifty-three Plymouth painted gray
and a green tree
wading into the metal
breaking around that tree,
while the driver lolled and flopped
his loose way back to babyhood,
an unstrung puppet of a child
who grew at last so young he died
into a heap of random limbs:
but it was sudden, done,
just stick-man, just new-made junk,
the official affairs of uniformed cars
and brushy voices out of radios;
so leaving it to those who clean it up,
I walked narrowly away,
stopping once to pick up someone's book
thrown open to the page with Melville's name
and academic poem of
matter and its ancient, brutal claim.

Bomb-shelter

When the clock broke, it was over.
Until its tinny cardiac, we'd managed,
one set against the other, to advance.
I threw it on the cans, north corner.
I stayed for what I think were three more days.
White noise on the radio. No change.
The bulb alone could not make day and night.
When walls became a problem, I got out.
I had to break the door. It is a day.
It still looks like it looked like when it hit.
The sea turned gray and silver as hacked lead.
The sky was sick with light.
The wind collapsed with sound and then was done.
My face was white and black, my brain a ball of glass.

Seconal

Twenty years, awake to every day;
the sun, its shock or sullenness of light,
darkness—pools and ditches of air;
so tired—twenty pills to sleep.
("Slap her! Make her walk! Talk to her!
She has to stay awake! Keep her awake!")
Their worry founders in her year-wide yawns,
her calm dilating in a snow of Seconal.
Myself as dumb and lost in drifts as she,
I wander to my room, stung
briefly by the siren as it comes,
but yawning then myself that I forget,
as she forgot herself, her in my smaller, shorter sleep.

January

Half in, half out of doorways,
always ghost and girl at once,
pale resonance with red hair,
she is gauche in anything not January,
puzzled at any kind of sun,
at any red-rimmed noon in day or man.
Afterwards asking "Did I do it right?"
as if fire were a craft, as if I
could teach rhythms of woman and man;
how lost her twenty lovers must have been—
such sadness in red hair, white skin.

It

Top Forty yells it out, but not this one:
I blush to say it, even think it,
even in our doubled secret dark,
safe from any ears but yours, two
very fine ears.
In all clench-jawed America,
no one says it,
as if it were the secret code,
and we bit tongues against Gestapo questions,
polite all-day, all-night questions.
It's after the secret hair sprouts that we lease it,
for our entire ever, to the radio.
Before that teen-age sign-away
I love you love we love us love love
conjugates everywhere on our childish tongues,
but about age twelve we start to suit the action,
and forget the word.
So if I never say I love you, it's not true.
I do.

      love

you

Illness

Oh I'm clever, clever. I
cannot die. What scintillance
of brain cells . . . Hell!—and fever, fever.
You shimmer quaintly, nurse. In or out
of phase, please. Really. You know,
I've half a mind . . . ho! Ice, I see.
By water burn my blaze away . . .

Most cold this morning, cold.
The sun is black, sucks
where it once spent its light,
August is reversed, and dust is snow.
I cannot quite remember, are you gone?
How far? From where do your letters come?
I do remember mornings when we two
rose with the sea breeze,
my shirt blown about on you,
time rewound with every wave.
That sun: will it never white again?
We wrote letters for a long time, long time, long time . . .
Distance shuts my mouth.

The mistral and sirocco yield:
I regain my weather and my weight.
I lie down late, rise early, often see
the round return of one more day.

The Distant

Those who are growing
easier as their hair goes gray,
those more distant everyday,
drinking shallowly and seldom,
eating nothing to speak of,
sleeping an hour before dawn,
and breathing a few times a day,
their eyes steadily empty with something
they learn as they forget the earth,
or rather, deal with it as it is;
how do we talk with such men?
How do we get them to tell
through their frail bodies and wrinkles
what they are the maze and puzzle and sign of?
Even with each other they won't tell,
but talk around the changes they've seen,
the celebrities they've seen
who are dead, the first Model A
and the bad roads, and the many friends
who are dead; so the younger
shake their heads and leave them to themselves;
for how can you deal with them,
be they ever so rich and strange,
if they do nothing but talk of change?

Death of a Football Star

Still arms will not hang straight;
they remember in cramps tonight how
with these limbs I lifted him,
huge, myself child to his man,
onto the cart, white sheets and wheels,
my ears jammed with ringing and silence,
the shouts of attendants unheard,
but then, ganged into a corner,
held hard from hurting the dead,
my ears returned with one sound:
the tick of bearings and clock
as they wheeled his huge stillness away.
Afterwards I was so clumsy,
all things were so slow afterwards.
In my hand the coffee cup rose,
weightless and drifting and white.
I drank once without any taste
and set the cup down for a year,
smashed it without any force,
and bled for forever until
a doctor prescribed pills to calm me,
who was calm as the form of my friend.

How Long

Some morning of knives and nausea,
at the cliff's edge in the kitchen,
scarring formica for a slice of bread
for my stomach to bite down on,
my time will be packed up,
free of forethought, and I
will put away the clock and eat,
in the yellow kitchen, my bread, and sleep.

You will be gone then, for good, good, good;
your porter, your redcap, old I
will have lugged the baggage out.
Will you tip me a kiss,
a quarter, will you smile,
wave and wave and wave a while?

When my red phone caught the rings,
I wouldn't treat it, I ignored it.
Better it sick than me sick.
But then "knock knock hello hello
I wouldn't come back but I love you so"
and you're in, unpacking you.
I wound the clock but didn't set it,
since all I care is how long.

At night you are always hot
to that side of me near you,
so I turn and turn, and I turn,
like a man on a spit, not to burn,
but be done, be done.

Child

At the top of the house tonight
in a room I once lived in,
the slant ceiling hunches over
and the square-shouldered doorway cants
his enormous empty body to my sight
and no angles are true: nothing obeys
the plumbline and tape; worn tile
warps in distress at hot and cold,
old windows of bad glass change the laws,
and there are strange animals, the alien toys
of a child, and there is the child smell:
have you ever heard them before they're human,
before we teach them everything?—have you ever
heard them?—they laugh like they're outside—
whole skull humming in their animal—
listen! we must make them human—
they could be these other things—I remember
through his bad glass when I wasn't human—
I remember when I was connected—
telephone and powerline, table and chair,
all, the chaos and the light, the whole,
hydrogen and helium,
the sun of total confusion.

Visiting Home: On My Father Awakening

She clicked on the light and shook him from his dream.
He woke up small in the scarred oak bed,
Eyes red with fighting the insistent hunger
That was the only danger in 1933
In Chippewa County; he woke up curled up,
Dream-caught, confused, broke open his small knot,
Bunched like a shot squirrel, and stretched stiffly.
"I know he's here, I know," he said, coming slowly
From those old forests, "I'm awake." But his eyes
Wouldn't come to today. The wide silence
Of the hunt held him, and he looked past us,
Intent, still searching trees for nests,
To find in all the green one small furred meal,
Some dark meat for the many who must feed
On the illegal rabbit, the unlawful squirrel,
For it was summer, and all game was out of season,
As if hunger had a season but to eat.
But no. I could not blind his eye-dark dream
With the electric bulb of 1966.
I turned away and I turned out the light.
I, who have never been bound to single-shot
And lead-shock for the daily sake of family,
Who killed perhaps ten bottles, and once, one slow squirrel,
Could not forbid him gun, trees, squirrel, hunger again,
Could not deny him his man-making pain.

Walking Fence

Many there are
who don't love a fence,
the fence Robert Frost
once walked in his thought
when he couldn't decide
either/or about walls.
Now I had a fence,
a white wooden fence
that I walked once,
with grass on one side,
and grass on the other,
its paint scaling off,
its leg-posts wobbly
where water had bitten
with the teeth of Wisconsin.
When I dared its blunt balance
with my thin-worn soles,
I walked the white wobble
for a hundred yards,
but I fell on my belly
like a sack on the fence,
then slowly slid off
like a sack on one grass,
where, empty of air,
I cried for air,
but I could get breath
enough for living
and maybe more fencing
only on coming
dizzy near dying.
That day I'd a bruise
on my round of a belly
to help me remember

that walking fence
is a serious business
when you're human and heavy,
so let someone tell you
who knows about fences,
that if you don't pick
one grass over another,
you'd better be ready
for a bruise on the belly,
a problem with breath,
and some tears.

To One Skeleton in One Indian Mound

At noon the sun like one more engine
roared overhead,
and all we amateurs at spades
crossed our broad blades in the heat
in the hurry to dig up and hoard,
but now . . . all your awry bones
and a round skull full of cobweb thought
unclock my day,
and the dig's quarrel of shovels
disappears. Let the others save and save
their bones against the dozers
bulling their way here and there tomorrow
to the tick. My thin friend,
I could outsit America,
spinning a headful of those subtle threads,
and in a jumble in the next time's mound
crook my head-house a thousand years
around the nebulae of webs,
thinking on the spinner's work of stars.

An Indigestible Dream

The damp of three summers' rotting rain
ruined the emperor's day with a cold,
and left the wheat-fields like paddys.
When the taxman added his tax that year,
he went off his diet with worry,
for the imperial pocket was short of full
about one new palace worth of dollars,
but descending heavily from his office
on the towns, he adjusted the towns.
Sullen farmers clotted the corners,
leisurely as the rich but more hungry,
angering the air with belly-growls,
but the taxman slid like a stick of butter
easily unhearing along the streets:
he must have gone deaf at the edge of town.
Knowing the business of government heavy,
and knowing the taxman a busy man,
the farmers, to get his attention,
threw stones, but the mayor's high walls
were hard of hearing as the official ear,
though the taxman couldn't have heard anyway,
for that buttery ear was being busily licked
by the confidential tongue of the mayor.
The taxman, back in the capital,
figured out one day that each farmer
had been taxed the cost of one stone, well-cut,
for that pocket-filling palace of dollars.
An indigestible dream that night,
a dream of farmers square as cut stones,
silent farmers, a whole palace of farmers,
woke up the taxman till nearly morning.

Secrets

Daily I bought him candy,
riding the bike we'd built from junk,
the bike that had three tires,
one on the front and two on back,
the two back tires with one inside the other,
so we could stagger holes against a blowout.
Daily I rode it to the neighbor grocery,
that had an old-time wooden floor
worn into pathways by years of feet,
there to buy three Hershey bars,
with or without nuts, like old Norm said,
smiling slyly at the embarrassed boy,
who didn't want to show he knew the joke.
Sometimes I didn't buy the Hersheys,
I hated the joking part so much,
sometimes I'd buy licorice,
but then grampa'd be mad,
for Hersheys were what he really liked.
I'd lie and tell him Norm was out,
and he'd eat second best, unsatisfied.
Always, though, I'd buy red soda,
a big bottle, because we both liked that,
then ride back home one-handed,
paper bag in the other arm,
pretending to go up or down a mountain,
depending on which gear I was in,
high or low, for second gear was broken.
He'd sit on the porch, on the left side sagging,
stick arms and legs and a big body,
almost like I'd drawn him once,
circle for body and lines for limbs,
like a boy will sometimes do.
Careful of mother, I'd come the back way,

on the dining-room side of the house,
for Hersheys and soda were secret things,
the kind of secret the old and young
will make against the big ones of the house.
It was more than that though, more than a secret,
though I never did quite know what was wrong,
why candy was bad, and why soda,
except it was something called insulin,
that happened at night, that I wasn't let watch,
that had something to do with little bottles
kept cool in the icebox, that I couldn't touch.
So we kept the secret that mother knew,
knew but overlooked each afternoon,
the secret really secret from my father,
who would have stopped my daily rides,
but an old and dying man's got to have something,
like she told me ten years later.
My anger at what she'd done outgrown,
and even outgrown my own guilt,
I've become almost proud of what I did,
that I rode the bike and bought the candy
to battle the insulin, maybe killing a little,
maybe taking some weeks from his months
with eight-years-old near ignorance
of how good candy could somehow be bad,
and I remember with no accusations
the learning about secrets, years ago.

The End

The shadows of the earth grow short,
For everything that is upstanding
Must soon be level in the sun.
The dialectic of the day and night
Collapses to a synthesis
In the numb medium of red twilight,
for everything that is of two
Must be one.
The slow untroubled circling of the moon
Goes frantic as it spirals in,
Bulges, breaks, and smashes all,
For everything that is in balance
Must fall.
And now, low in the dim sky, the red sun,
That has consumed itself for time
And fed all the hungers of the earth,
Will settle the sum of no and yes,
And briefly incandesce.

Other Poems

Dreams

Her dream was gentle hands, a winning smile,
and eyes as bluely fair as skies,
not hard arms and taking hands
to make her suddenly wise.
But her daydream fled with her attacker,
who now feared screams that didn't come,
for she had opened to her deeper dream
when she began to move with him.

Sailing

I set the sea shell in a port tack,
but in primitive rage against my sailing,
the green infuriate hammers of the sea
beat the boat dazed as its white fragility
was bombarded repeatedly by the savage waves,
and the wind slammed deep in the thin sail,
its frail order weakening under the convulsed battering,
until the boat bent, bowed toward the water, hovering, until
the sail rived with a scream to upright me.

Collapse

The stage floor is worn thin,
the actors mince across the boards in dread,
and even the audience knows their parts too well,
but if the whole theater should collapse,
newspapers would merely flitter from the press
and experts merely analyze and guess,
concluding; "It was ill-designed, perhaps—
but I can't commit myself to why it fell.
The new one won't be better—like I've always said,
Those old building codes are a sin."

Hill-climb

Rutting the wheel-way up,
storm of sand and rock,
break this bike or make it, dammit,
drive, you headlamped devil,
burst earth at hilltop,
arc and bottom, dig, dig,
stand in second gear
and go devour wind with steel,
destroy the need for speed or die.

for my father

my father wrote in flesh,
on white, parting parchment,
on supple and yielding skin
tightened for him.

he knew nothing of what he did
in that dark-liquid bed;
erect in his man-power,
he wrote in mindless words.

he knew nothing of what he did,
but to him I have no need
to lie forgiveness—he needs none,
for his words have a ringing sound.

his chromosomes were keyed
into a sunly code,
his words aligned the atoms
of a galing, windly mind,

and he unlocked the door
that blocked the watery shaft
so I could break the surface
with bones curved of his pen.

he knew nothing of what he did,
but it was good,
and as I laugh in light
my flesh sings of his words.

sun

when understanding burns away the mist,
sunhigh revelation in the noon of joy,
pain-brilliance fevers think to feel,
flares an inside twisting out to everywhere
through miraculous topology;
openness and sun are now.

Seven

In dawn's first-laugh fireburst,
When Logic slips in dewy grass
And stains his knees a skipping green,
My number is seven in a new breeze,
My mind is soda-pop bubbles,
My body a plastic delight.

A supercharged seven of hearts throatpurrs
My motorcycle along the walks,
Snarls it down the steepest hill,
And sun-shout days clatter by,
A picket run along a picket fence
That runs a million miles—

Until he stands erect, and stiffly
Brushes nonsense from his clothes.

Monody: One Madam to Another

Madam Earth, you're more a whore than I am.
I've stood on my head, turned somersaults,
anything for a customer with a big fat tip,
but you've turned more tricks than ever I did,
for you turn away no man.
In the end you box us all, even me,
man or woman's no difference to you,
you've got to take it and take it in,
but what makes you the final whore—
you won't take cash and let us go;
for we pay everything we've got.
So all I've got to say is there've been times,
times I spread for free,
and they liked it,
and were at peace, alive, in me.

The Script

The old man rehearsing my flesh
broke my legs to bring me down;
under the shower, in the pin-hot rain,
my knees thumped porcelain, twin thrown logs;
I slumped downhill to dream, undone,
darkly remembering the flesh I am,
from father and mother, by their first cell,
the human river knotted to a child,
untied a lifetime to that dying man
swelling the river's run as he forgets
back to the water the part he knows too well.
After child and before old man,
halfway from river to river,
I am my middleman and must learn
my script that's written in each cell,
draining myself through my design,
that, coming at end to my untie,
I have performed entirely.

The Harsh In Music

You have been true, and I promiscuous,
If those quaint words define the modern way,
When one or many's a matter of choice
And why not seems as reasonable as why;
So I've an intimate crowd who've never stayed
Except in certain ghostly whispered thoughts,
Until I found the snakey chorus loud,
And wished I'd stopped at ten or so one-nights;
While you, in your unmarried faithfulness,
Have found one instrument a monotone,
And thinking three years' love a two years' loss,
Now want instead a symphony of men.
But what is harsh in music is while I
Am your one more, you're not one less for me.

Song of the Wandering Jew

I am the Wandering Jew,
I struck at Christ with a closed fist
As I struck at Baal and Osiris,
And it makes no difference.

I have no memory of why
I am the keeper of balance,
Alternate Christ and Anti-Christ,
But it makes no difference.

You know as well as I
Of the worth of arguments,
But they must go on for some time,
Since it makes no difference.

But when it is all in balance,
A white noise of the mind,
I am mindless with that waterfall
Which makes no difference.

To Labour for the Wind

And what profit hath he
That hath laboured for the wind?
For who can search for it and find,
And what man hold its brief breath;
It is more transient than snow,
Which in one small hour is gone.
And a man who had the need,
Where would he search?
What is the source of it,
And what the end;
For even as it comes from nowhere,
It goes also to nowhere;
For it has no North or South,
No East or West,
But abides equally with all of these,
And is one with the child and the old man.

On My Father Awakening Shouting

But can I shoot away that doubt,
Demobilize the enemy, distending lead
To prove the punch behind my hollow point,
Confirming with the bang the wavering good?
But can I escape, can I escape
The very palpable recoil of such a hit,
The question magnified behind the scope
As I dismantle my own man? The hurt
That heals in daylight gapes in dreams.
No gun kills as surely as it seems.

Tablets

I would like to know why David Roberts
sold her the one bottle of white tablets
and wouldn't sell her two.
Was he afraid to do what she was not,
or did he want to keep a customer
for another try on some night later,
or—did he plan some leisurely delight?
Whatever: she's not through,
and must repeat her purchase, buy again—
I wish he'd sold her two and got it done.

Earth

Always the long push and pull of blood,
always the building up, and collapse of lungs,
always the mass of flesh to overcome,
obese inertia and base momentum,
but always too beyond all these there is
the continuing earth,
which outwears all its thousand forms to one
equally beyond the fatigue of fine steel
and the water-weariness of stone.
This night, whisper-spent and eye-bleared-out
in a clock-watched and hour-exhausting
hushed soliloquy in sibilance, ends but in earth,
which calms all that crackle of the nerves,
and submits us to the summer sun
'til we admit, brought to that calm,
the snow of flesh, the ice of bones.

Wrist-watch

Unwind your coiled cold,
your ice-tight sleety machine;
the clock-shock of its minute tick
but wakes me to the wrist-bound world,
but wakes me to my three-named enemy:
time, December, and the ticking wind.
And therefore thanks to you my trinity,
my three-personed implacable cold God:
with eyes as open as the handcuff's closed
I can now find that woman that
driven by the sprung whirlwind
we coil in our own Spring.

Speech

Let them come heavily, bull-boned men
who kill with many blows of a blunt stone
determinedly, because they do not understand:
these men can be yoked neck and neck,
their tongues are numb, they are not to be feared;
if ever they discover speech, their speech
will move with the tide by sun and moon.
No, fear, but fear the efficiently thin,
the light and bright as aluminum,
the neon-tongued, who have teeth of movable type
and squawk from a nylon voicebox
words that are to them as paper cups,
paper plates, plastic knives, plastic forks.

No More

That a woman should so live for today
that I am now to her like food long eaten,
used, built into the body, and forgotten,
though a month ago we together cried "today,"
and wound a double helix of the limbs:
at this I shout at those two in the park tonight,
startling them closer, crazy man out of the night:
"There is this much and there is no more:
There is tonight and there is tomorrow!"

Florida April

The summer's coal-long twilight glow
and the loafing floating ash of stars:
April, where April is the cruelest month—
here—just June, machine-green palms,
and heavy traffic on the highway north.
Today another died. As nurses aide
for the unimportant terminal ward,
I was the old man's friend for his last gasps.
With the final loss of breath through strength squandered,
he told me how it is at eighty-one.
"Always the long push and pull of blood,
always the building up, and collapse of lungs,
always the mass of flesh to overcome,
obese inertia and base momentum,
but always too beyond all these there is
the continuing earth,
which outwears all its thousand forms to one
equally beyond the fatigue of fine steel
and the water-weariness of stone."

Learn

Skin is forbidden again—
not to touch! not to touch!
forget each history of wet,
for we are what reverses lust,
and makes a ghost of red memory.
Again there is "I meant . . ." "I didn't mean . . ."
two talk at once or not at all,
and all tends to Philosophy.
But how long can we walk and talk,
and rarefy our night and day,
how long can we practice innocence
when hunger tells us to turn in,
lose everything but what we only are,
and learn what is forgotten once again.

untitled (Now divide the unit world in two)

. . . Now divide the unit world in two
and call these twins habitual day and night;
assign to one the dream that works our rest,
and to the other, memory—this done,
this is a man: born one, grown up two,
a double citizen of neighbor countries,
each foreign across the border to his other,
although each whole to his own eye.
What then when a man must meet his states,
and at the junction of his day and night combust
the singular fire of a sun and moon
when he makes these twin lights twilight? . . .

Letter to Ward A

That added-on, crazy-quilt clash of a house
might have been our stitched-together marriage:
split shakes and logs for the ground floor
and a second floor clapboard and plywood.
The nights when you left upstairs and me,
spiraling down two flights to the cellar,
I'd try, but I couldn't remember
if you were worse at the other house.
A wide hall pinched to a small door,
three kinds of windows in one long wall,
none of it foursquare or true,
it must have helped odd-angle you.
Worst of it was for me those nights
when you played the house from that cellar:
hot water, then cold, lights off and on,
the steam heat hissing and whistling,
and all of it in patterns and design,
until sometimes I had to crouch in bed,
half-afraid to half-understand.
The meters with their needles, ducts,
the pilot lights and the valves, all things
half-magical to a wife anyway,
even before the patterns began.
But then, an hour or hours later,
everything would go on at once,
and you'd dull-foot your way upstairs,
again a man of right-angle mind.
You had to go to that place, I guess,
especially after that last long night,
when the lights blew out and I found you,
mind-dark, with your hands in the fusebox,
but I miss the music now—so intricate!
and with such an unlikely instrument.

The Reasoning Rock

If a rock could think,
I mean a brain-round rock,
to make its thinking easier,
(and maybe ponder is better than think,
for a rock must think ten million years,
long pondering, about one thing,)
but anyway, if a rock could think,
about the date of the dawn of Superman,
this reasoning rock would say, Q.E.D.,
"What top-speed Keystone Kops were men!"

Sub for Sail

If I didn't pay rent I'd be a ghost,
a bump in the night
for the other tenants to whisper about,
but once a week Landlady docks,
half steamed-up on Irish Mist,
hand out for me to unhand cash,
and I buy off the all-outdoors
for another seven days.
But every week, before her bon voyage,
she puts me on the stand,
crossly examining the cluttered room:
"Why were you on the night of the day
reading all night?" she says.
I fold my hands. I clear my throat. I say
(lying) "I am" "Perjury
is an ugly word," she says.
"writing a book on" I say.
"Perjury, Sir."
"di-proto-astro-negativity."
and she leaves.
I close the hatch and dive,
cruising my book-pile,
discoursing with dolphins and whales
about the Marianas Trench,
about our common full fathom five,
snoring an hour on Monday,
Tuesday half a day,
reading toward and sleeping away my time
in a deepsea June or July,
for it's hot down here, the pressure's on,
more and more I need some air.
Next time the S. S. Weekly nears the door,
I think I'll trade my sub for sail,

exit the harbor, come about,
and gathering a deep canvas of air,
I'll up on the water, and away from here,
to see how is the all-out-there.

For Grandfather, Dying Hard

Old man, coughing your way half here, back
far enough from death to see the surface,
thick with those who bother to breathe air,
die, float off in the dark and disappear
beyond all sonar but my memory.
What makes you think you can still live here,
your huge heart thin as a red balloon,
shaking your body like a distant bomb-blast?
But most of all I hate your eyes, their fear.

The Ends of the Bed

I took this ball of dirt the world
for heaven and hell;
the water of nerves a woman gives,
hunger, a bank account:
these things were solid as sunlight.
I went to and back, I worked,
slept deep, fulfilled my every day,
and I lived in the house of the whole big world.
Now the whole big world is starved of weight,
that house has fallen in a flat of cards.
We're like some storybook ragpaper keeps,
some Hansel and Gretel thing of scares
to nightmare children into sleep;
all this pother of day and night,
the white sheet red with the child,
wet with the middleman
as he reforms his flesh,
bloody again with the old man's lungs,
none of it seems more than breath.
Why, seventy years are crammed in an hour:
marriage and career, financial empire, death
and it's all a story to start the night,
between the first and last of breath,
between the ends of the bed.

Night-light

The night-light burns its angry, hungry red,
ravening the night fast as my sleepless
saving; if it can eat at this red rate,
awakening is false and sleeping true,
time and its savage dream of light a lie,
and dream dark fact to its pale fantasy.
So dream: in the still pool beneath the mind,
lose all our wear of days, our loss of nights.
Forget deep as the ape—no! to the fish—
farther, to the cell, back until the clock
drowns in the sea by which we swarm and live,
our memory in genes, our reason that we breathe,
our understanding oxygen and light.
And the result? Drowned daily into calm,
we sink but to awake, shock of sun or night,
and there the ticking or the humming clock.

And I Fear

In silos and cradles, carefully cool,
air-conditioned, checked continually,
watched and tended by technicians,
our stockpiles wait the one-time call
that speeds them and converts them
from mere matter webbed with circuitry
to a local, uncontrollable sun.

The triggered clock cuts off the dark
and all the nightmares of the other side and
Pop! my mushroom of a brain blooms again,
dewy and ready to be sucked dry all day.
The sun, its hardly dangerous soft radiation on,
sweats me from my limbo and I see,
the unstable room still solid
in its unexploded light.
My day gapes before me like the door,
opening on all the world I have, still there,
reprieve granted from the final heat.

I am an outpatient, a man qualified
by certain drugs. It took shock
to fry me from my neutral stall,
but, all that Brownian motion stopped,
I'm turned loose on the world,
bracketed by a pair of pills
setting my upper, my lower bounds.

In my kitchen, the stove-snake cooks my food,
and at night its split electric tongue
dangles the apple by which I wait to sleep,
for I was born to the broadcast radiation,
and Big Boy's ghost fell out into my bones,

sighing in my marrow its long decay,
forshortening my half-life until I knew
this is the morning I will live or die.

It was in the army, in Japan,
at Hiroshima I lost my common sense,
and stopped for all my personal time
being numb with the millions of the expected dead.
The museum there has uncommon stones
stamped with the shadows of that summer's leaves,
and still the people of the city say
how some are never either sick or well,
and others, cut, don't heal:
I puzzled doctors at the base
by waiting awake for several days;
when my white blood-count went low,
they flew me back,
amazed at what the mind can do:
DISCHARGED

My static still low enough to work,
I took a job in some big building,
filing away my forty hours and more,
in an alphabetical sub-basement room,
but through the walls of files
I felt the background radiation rise,
and when I filed schematics
for the sixteenth sub-assembly of a missile,
to get away from the geiger's roar,
I jammed my nerves to one
white noise of a neural snow
and nothing did me any good or any harm.

Burnt out of that and six feet tall again,
I rattle between the ups and downs,
bracketed by a pair of pills
setting my upper, my lower bounds.
Before the bar of that double governor,
my range and domain were all the short way
to the near end of human time,
and though the leveling drug
has landscaped me to relative calm,
nothing can trick the final eye,
the ear that's tuned to the coming sun,
the nerves set for the heat:
I see walls fail,
my skin reads radiation everywhere,
in the mushroom of my brain I hear
the hydrogen's confusion,
the helium's crisp answer
and I fear.

2-S

Day breaks in the afternoon,
the spine is gone, we're paralyzed.
The evasions approach zero
as a limit.
What to talk about today,
what to avoid?
Nothing, I'm afraid.
Remember the one of us
who didn't make it through boot camp
because he didn't want to,
but shut-the-fuck-up-soldier for good?
In a place like that
he couldn't sleep the twenty hours a day
that let him stay awake at all,
and had to get it some way.
The camp commandant,
one of those one-eyed men
who charges through the world
damn-well getting his duties done,
wrote us a brisk letter
about how anyone
who didn't want to bang a gun in 'Nam
wasn't a man anyway.
I wasn't convinced,
and the funeral wasn't fun.
I myself am tired of late,
and my 2-S runs out soon.
I hope at least I get a different camp
from his one.

Boot-camp Suicide

In the cinder-block shack
of my dormitory room,
I sleep to dream and wake up to remember
how one of us has failed boot camp,
standing like the man his sergeant made him,
upright on the obstacle course,
then machine-gunned down,
flunked out of breath and blood.
His death is foursquare fact,
cramped as a slot in a basement dorm,
but his memory exceeds him
as the world inflates their dime-store dolls
so the staff shrink on Uncle's team
can sign him off to hell, Case Closed
by a penetrating pen,
while the local pump of the underground press
types him into heaven.
Before he failed his mid-terms here on earth
and passed his physical,
I was his roommate once, and I know
nothing except that barracks and reveille
would break the twenty hours a day
he had to sleep to stay awake at all,
and I know from a photograph
how bad his khaki fit.

Sunday

The mower woke us, motor throbbing
through the room, then dying . . . sigh, turn over,
the blur of a close face, the touch—
blossoming into morning, light opens
to laughter as we wake to being human,
sculpt ourselves in sheet, and talk
of what to do on Sunday in such light;
then standing in a motion in her simple skin,
she walks to the kitchen, makes coffee, singing,
serves willingly where no one would command;
finished waking, we dress lightly, leave,
confirm through morning and the day
our ancient, nightly trust of two asleep.

Shark

Out of my room, cool with motor and coil
for my daily lifelong dream,
hammerhead shark bites down
white from his exploding brain!
Never a fish this fierce
from any seventh sea! Space
only has fathom enough for fire this free, we
only, and sometimes, eyes enough to see.

After Much Speech

Silence after much speech; it is right,
caught up here now out of common time,
in the crystalline once tense of poetry,
that we—he, you, and I, the three the one
that wrote and sings these constant, ancient lines,
shall shiver, the book close, and we two choose
to fall into the flesh and lose our voice.

untitled (I awake so easily today)

I awake so easily today
as if awakening were breathing out
the night's long breathing in . . .
and she—sleeps, still taking breath,
as easily as morning's light
grows in its ancient, patient way.
In this broken cabin,
equally of land and sea,
on sand between the collapsing and collapsed,
we live our lifelong doorway,
waiting out the tide when it takes hold,
worrying the pilings,
not eager to take hold, just there,
the random fact of eventual capture.

But no tide now, just wind
rustling the brown palmetto fronds
casting their moving maze on us,
a maze of shadows she accepts,
as calm as milk-glass under them.

On our first morning, how I worried:
would she be able to be with me,
at once forgetting and remembering
her other first mornings with others?
She undressed to the sadness of nakedness,
in the old confusion of twilight,
in the old understanding,
clothes falling softly as her breathing,
and then came,
forgetting and remembering.

If we had waited, been deliberate,
entering a maze of yes and no
to find some certain yes or no,
to find some law besides the Second Law . . .
O that wish!
to enter it, turn face up, and then
O to rise!
above the timebound maze
in the noon's discovering blaze
and see the pattern, the whole pattern!
O to rise
          if we could but rise,
leave these doors
and corridors—

But she stirs—"Good morning."
Good morrow to you now as now you come,
good morrow as we now say yes again
for yes we will go down,
caught in the center,
we will go down
to join the beginning and the end,
to obey the timebound order of the land,
to become the strict disorder of the sea.

untitled (two riddles)

Done

1.   Its way with people is to break;
Its tool the sun, or anything;
Its patience is in brevity;
Its aim, to get things Done;
Its paradox—that I took some
To write this riddle, but used up none.

Marriage

2.   The positive and negative
must mate their alternating charge
inside a bulb and not at large
for any lasting light to live.

Downtown Dealer

Resume
    B.A.: 1959.
    M.A.: 1961.
    Married: 1960.
    Taught three years: Philosophy
    At a minor university.
    1963: Wife died: suicide.
    One day in 1964,
    In a lecture on reality,
    To everything I said
    There echoed refutations in my head.

But this New Job is Really Me
    it's really fine it's mine
    the chrome's so bright it's like clear thought
    the motors roar like chimera
    it's just the thing
    it's just the way it all should be
    my salesman's tongue as slippery
    as any salesman's tongue can be
    from years of lectures on philosophy
    and since it is so really good
    I'm here to stay
    I'm here to sell it everyday
    I do it any way I can
    you see those flashing reds and greens?
    A SALE A DAY   A SALE A DAY
    the neons really pull them in
         A SALE A DAY
    everyday some guy comes in
    machinists hands cut up like meat
    I put him in the driver's seat
    it costs him "seven dollars weekly"

it costs me what I have to pay
A SALE A DAY
a man who buys his time by sales
has to buy the only way
has to buy it everyday
or go under

So I will make a deal
any kind of deal
Hey mister see that two-tone Ford
gray and pink as dawn?
I will make a real deal
You know that dream you have of dawn?
I can make it real
I can make it real real
if I can make it.

Of Archibald MacLeish

At last, growing brown into his end,
The straight man bends to the fire,
The good liar enters what he lies about,
And finally lives out his poems about age
As its impersonal rage burns him down.

Shrapnel

As I lie here lightly
crumbled in the moon,
I must laugh gently.
I used to be so stiff, thinking of tonight,
all mechanical arms and lead-lined containers.
I guess I thought I could dump it
in some out-of-the-way spot and forget it.
But now I find no need —
I hold my metal in me like a child
and know its warmth like a mother,
from the inside.

Mapping the Terrain

An acid-head friend of mine,
his eyes unfocused on infinity,
came by one day for a month or two,
talking of highways and freeways,
and how he's locked in America,
since our north and south neighbors' border guards
gate the tourists but fence the longhairs out.

Alterly he thumbs and sits,
ranging America in my little room,
but trying to cross at my kitchen door
into Canada, he's scissored off:
the Mounted Police, Stan Laurel style,
like body-political practical nurses,
jockey their jodhpurs, and judge him a germ,
so he hitches south to my easychair—
and a second cut-short border halt
for an Oliver Hardy Federale.

Yet as he tours the Fifty States,
the stops and goes of his travels
are all somehow the same,
as if his stasis were a kind of motion,
his motion some strange stand,
like water running the river still,
or the whirlpool turning in its rest;
but how can someone rest as he moves,
or be in action as he is still?

And his eyes! Though he sees,
he seems to look at nothing,
as though the world were so much windowglass,
and he more giving the light than taking in.

This Keystone Kops matter of keys
to lock him in and out and up
bars and borders him not at all:
plainly he could live in this one room,
less my vast frontier of kitchen,
and think himself unbounded Lord and King.
Such ease! Is it the etch of the acid
has razed the nerve-noise in the head
and incandesced his brain,
or was the easy, day-light man
scripted in his primitive cell,
never to suffer a tape-loop of the mind?

Melville, if Hawthorne saw it right,
had no rest from Mind:
on open beach, he so amazed beach sand
with his brooding toward and from,
you would have thought him cabined there,
yet his only bulkheads were the north and south.

Moses broke water out of a rock,
and Jacob fought the white shadow of God:
had Melville that staff or that angel,
he might have drunk and lost to faith,
rather than shift dry sand,
a thirty-years thirsting man along the salt.
Instead fixed fate, free will, foreknowledge absolute
were like the Mojave sun: he,
in a heat-stroke of these themes,
cracked his brain like desert mud,
and to learn what? that desert thought
could only shine black the man's shadow
in which the Pequod and Moby Dick went down.

World-sailor Melville, landlocked in thought,
and my everywhere sunshine friend
between them have split the unit sun:
heat, salt heat, for the sailor,
for my friend all light, all delight,
but I both sweat and see,
and I both thirst and drink.

To hitchhike lightly through highway U.S.A.,
all-unthinking, and as birds of the air,
is not enough man; it brackets us:
it's too much God and too much animal;
but to pace in the sun and syllogize fixed fate
is to look for your own eyes:
fixed fate is a riverbed,
free will an abundant water,
foreknowledge absolute the river-land:
old Aristotle and his logic box,
unless you walk, swim, and wade this terrain,
are the organ-grinder and organ of the mind,
and a man, that metaphysical mud,
who maps, and thinks the map the terrain,
is terrain-mocked as he cranks the Ergo tune:
as the riverbed shapes the river,
the river recuts the bed;
what are our maps, if each alter the other?

A Footnote to the Alexandrian Fire

The high-heaped books of Alexandria,
reaching critical mass, fire up,
and the PhD's get third degree burns
so Minimus the Grammarian
can save his gloss on Minor.
Stoke the galleries, scholars,
shovel the stacks like coal,
and quit your hydrant of tears:
not even the downleveling ardor of Troy
freed so much hot air.
Plato, if he could have seen this fire,
though a hard-bound man himself,
would have danced like Dionysus,
drunk with disglossing the Ideal Text,
several removes more near to the Real.
And about the texts, old sirs—
Alexandrian epics on the crash of Troy,
do you think them worth the burns?
Helen will be stolen, Troy burn,
Achilles die through a million rhymes,
though Alexandria were not.
If you must have texts though, I've got a few,
and you can fill up the margins, if you like,
though I've not much more than a common Homer,
and a few short pieces by memory.
I cannot unremember the ones I love.
Tell me—do you really value
books there's only one copy of?

WILLIAM HEDRINGTON was born in Chippewa Falls, Wisconsin, in 1947 and raised by his aunt and uncle, Earl and Clara Hedrington. After his graduation from Pius XI High School in Milwaukee, he enrolled in New College, an experimental college in Sarasota, Florida. He graduated from New College in 1970 and spent a year at Stanford University on a Wallace E. Stegner Fellowship in Creative Writing in Poetry. He was a student in Syracuse University's graduate program in creative writing at the time of his death in an automobile crash on October 31, 1971. During his lifetime, Hedrington's poems appeared in *Antioch Review*, *Armadillo*, *Westigan Review of Poetry,* and other magazines. Literary critic Cleanth Brooks, Gray Professor of Rhetoric at Yale University, expressed confidence that Hedrington would "soon make his mark as one of the best poets of his generation." *On the Downhill Side* is the first collection of Hedrington's poems in book form.

MICHAEL SMITH grew up in Henderson, Kentucky, and graduated from New College in 1970, the same year as Bill Hedrington. After Hedrington's death, he was entrusted by the family with the task of producing an edition of Hedrington's work. A strong proponent of dead languages, Smith studied Old English, Old French, and Latin at New College and continued his studies at the University of Chicago and the Dublin Institute for Advanced Studies, with romps through Old Norse, Old Irish, medieval Welsh, Old Icelandic, ancient Greek, Provençal, biblical Hebrew, and other dialects too numerous to mention. Smith now makes his living in the computer business. He lives in the Upper West Side of Manhattan, with his wife of eighteen years, Eve Wolfsohn, son Andrew Smith and daughter Emma Wolfsohn, and a large number of dusty books. Smith is an enthusiastic amateur musician and takes great pride in being the carillonneur of St. Martin's Church in the heart of Harlem.